IMAGES OF WAR

ARMOURED WARFARE
IN
NORTHWEST EUROPE
1944–1945

D1613285

Closing in on the Third Reich. Fighting its way down a German street is an M4A3(76mm) HVSS and its supporting infantry.

IMAGES OF WAR

ARMOURED WARFARE IN NORTHWEST EUROPE 1944–1945

RARE PHOTOGRAPHS FROM WARTIME ARCHIVES

Anthony Tucker-Jones

Pen & Sword
MILITARY

First published in Great Britain in 2013 by
PEN & SWORD MILITARY
an imprint of
Pen & Sword Books Ltd,
47 Church Street,
Barnsley,
South Yorkshire
S70 2AS

A CIP record for this book is available from the British Library.

ISBN 978 178159 175 8

Typeset by CHIC GRAPHICS

Printed and bound by CPI Group (UK) Ltd, Croydon, CR0 4YY

Pen & Sword Books Ltd incorporates the Imprints of
Pen & Sword Aviation, Pen & Sword Family History, Pen & Sword Maritime, Pen & Sword Military, Pen & Sword Discovery, Wharncliffe Local History, Wharncliffe True Crime, Wharncliffe Transport, Pen & Sword Select, Pen & Sword Military Classics, Leo Cooper, The Praetorian Press, Remember When, Seaforth Publishing and Frontline Publishing.

For a complete list of Pen & Sword titles please contact
Pen & Sword Books Limited
47 Church Street, Barnsley, South Yorkshire, S70 2AS, England
E-mail: enquiries@pen-and-sword.co.uk
Website: www.pen-and-sword.co.uk

Contents

Introduction

On the very eve of D-Day General Dwight D. Eisenhower, the Allied commander, issued a leaflet to every serviceman involved saying:

You are about to embark upon the Great Crusade, toward which we have striven these many months. The eyes of the world are upon you. The hopes and prayers of liberty-loving people everywhere march with you. In company with our brave Allies and brothers-in-arms on other Fronts, you will bring about the destruction of the German war machine, the elimination of Nazi tyranny over the oppressed peoples of Europe, and security for ourselves in a free world.

Your task will not be an easy one. Your enemy is well trained, well-equipped and battle-hardened. He will fight savagely.

Thus began the crusade to liberate Nazi-occupied Europe. The fierce battles fought in Northwest Europe during 1944-45 were a decisive phase of the Second World War and saw American, British, Canadian and Polish armoured divisions spearhead the assault on Adolf Hitler's Third Reich. Tanks were required to fight in the claustrophobic hedgerows of Normandy, the mud and waters of the Seine, Scheldt and Rhine rivers and the forests and snows of the Ardennes and the cities of Nazi Germany. These battles also saw the deployment of specialized amphibious armoured fighting vehicles first used in the Pacific war.

This book is designed to provide a photographic guide to armoured warfare in the Northwest Europe campaign and forms part of the Images of War series on armoured warfare by the author. This fighting featured a series of key armoured engagements, as well as three major armoured amphibious assaults conducted under a variety of different climatic and geographic conditions. In particular, the Scheldt and Rhine crossings required the deployment of specialized vehicles such as the Buffalo, DUKW, Weasel and Terrapin.

The armoured warfare conducted in Northwest Europe was characterized principally by a series of battles to overcome the continent's major rivers. Initially, following the D-Day landings in June 1944, the Allies struggled to get over the Orne north and south of Caen. This culminated in a major British defeat when the Germans halted three armoured divisions trying to cut their way east of the city.

Panzergruppe West thwarted General Montgomery's Operation Goodwood and inflicted 5,500 casualties and destroyed over 400 tanks for the loss of over 100 panzers.

It was only when the Americans broke out to the west that the German defences were finally compromised and they fought a desperate rearguard action on the River Dives in late August. The Allies then raced to the Seine, where they had to overcome another German rearguard at Rouen. Allied plans to hasten the end of the war came unstuck when the attempt to reach the Rhine in the Netherlands was defeated. This delayed securing the vital port of Antwerp and resulted in the brutal battle for the Scheldt. The Germans then launched a panzer counter-offensive to try to reach the bridges over the Meuse in an attempt to recapture Antwerp. In the closing months of the war the Allies launched their last major offensive, with their armoured assault over the mighty Rhine.

After Falaise General Montgomery reasoned: 'We should, therefore, stage a powerful thrust, preferably up the coastal plain, which must keep on and on without pause, so that the Germans never get time to draw breath. We shall then be able to bounce a crossing of the Rhine before they get their defences organised. We can encircle the Ruhr from the north, cut it off from Germany, and the war will then be over.' However, the exhausted 9th SS and 10th SS Panzer Divisions successfully stopped Montgomery's attempt to swiftly end the war and the Allies reverted to their plodding broad-front strategy across Western Europe.

The Allies substituted the Germans' daring Blitzkrieg with a strategy of roll-back based largely on superior firepower and numbers. Since the failure of Operation Market Garden, Supreme Allied Commander General Dwight Eisenhower remained averse to risking his flanks. The Germans could not understand why the Allied advance was so laborious and on such a broad front.

Despite the collapse at Falaise, Hitler was able to organize a massive counterstroke against the Allies to grab back the initiative. He intended to punch his armour through the lightly-defended Ardennes region in Belgium and seize Antwerp. This was not to be some feeble counter-attack, but a full-blown counter offensive using two whole reconstituted panzer armies.

Hitler massed twenty-eight divisions totalling some 275,000 men, 950 armoured fighting vehicles and 1,900 pieces of artillery for the Ardennes offensive in mid-December 1944. His generals wanted to restrict their goal to Liège, but he ruled the panzers must reach Antwerp. It was a race against time and the weather; once the snow-laden skies cleared Allied fighter-bombers inevitably wrestled back the initiative. Hitler's panzers were stopped in their tracks and then sent reeling.

The Rhineland was the scene of two costly campaigns in the closing months of the war. The US 1st Army fought from September 1944 through to February 1945 clearing German forces from the Hurtgen Forest, losing 24,000 men in the process. The Allies then geared themselves up to reach and subsequently cross the Rhine itself.

Although the Allies assessed that the Wehrmacht was in disarray, they had been very shaken by Hitler's surprise Ardennes offensive and subsequent tough fighting in the Hurtgen and Reichswald. In addition, with Montgomery in charge, assaulting the Rhine was another set-piece battle. The preparations for the crossing took two weeks, which many felt unnecessary. The Americans were particularly unhappy with Montgomery's cautious preparations and meticulous planning. While they were getting ready the 47th Panzer Corps was able to recoup in the Netherlands and the Germans were able to improve their defences. For the push across the Rhine, Montgomery wanted the 2nd Canadian Army's 2nd Corps and the US 9th Army's 16th Corps to be allocated to the British 2nd Army. The Americans objected and this led to the parallel Operation Flashpoint.

In late March 1945 the Allies crossed Germany's last major defensive barrier – the Rhine. After Operation Overlord this was the second largest operation undertaken by the British Army during the entire war. Fortunately for the Allies Montgomery decided to attack upstream of Emmerich, where the British 2nd Army faced the weakened German 1st Parachute Army, which had no panzers. Once the Allies were over the Rhine Hitler's panzers were a completely spent force, with the survivors surrendering in the Ruhr pocket.

Photograph Sources

The images in this book have been sourced by the author from various archive sources including the US Army and US Signal Corps, as well as the author's own considerable collection. Readers interested in the D-Day landings and the fighting in Normandy may wish to consult the author's companion volume *Images of War: Armoured Warfare in the Normandy Campaign*, also published by Pen & Sword.

Chapter One

Bourguébus Ridge

Following the D-Day landings on 6 June 1944, American forces fought to secure the port of Cherbourg while the British and Canadian armies battled to take the Norman capital Caen. Operation Goodwood, launched at 0745 on 18 July, employing the British 7th, 11th and Guards armoured divisions, was intended to seize the strategic high ground south of the city held by three panzer divisions. In their path lay a series of stone-built villages amidst hedge-lined fields and orchards. The Bourguébus Ridge was to prove a bloody tank graveyard.

General von Obstfelder's 86th Corps was supported by the 21st and 1st SS Panzer Divisions, while the 12th SS at Lisieux constituted the 1st SS Panzer Corps' reserve. In addition Tigers of the 503 and 101 SS Heavy Panzer Battalions were also available. The 1st SS were in reserve at Falaise, way to the south of Caen when Goodwood was launched, between Eterville and Mondeville, and were directed eastward towards Cagny. Subsequently the 1st SS and 12th SS were redeployed to the south and east of Caen on a line from Bras-Bourguébus-Frénouville-Emiéville, while 21st Panzer lay between Emiéville and Troarn along with the Tiger tanks.

The British assessed the German defences to be to a depth of three miles, when in fact generals Rommel and Eberbach had built five defensive zones covering ten miles. The first consisted of the infantry, then sixty tanks from 21st Panzer and thirty-nine Tigers; a chain of fortified villages and then the artillery on a gun line including the Garcelles-Secqueville woods and the Bourguébus Ridge, supported by panzergrenadiers and Panther tanks from the 1st SS. The final zone comprised two kampfgruppen from the 12th SS.

British intelligence severely underestimated the German defences, which were supported by 230 panzers, although including other armoured fighting vehicles this force totalled nearly 400. The initial defences, comprising the 16th Luftwaffe Field Division and 21st Panzer's inadequate assault gun battalion, were unlikely to hold up the British tanks for any length of time, especially once they had been pulverized by the Allied bomber fleets. Therefore the German defence relied on the panzergrenadiers of Kampfgruppe von Luck, drawn from the 21st Panzer.

The powerful German gun line on the Bourguébus ridge included seventy-eight

88mm guns, 194 field guns, twelve heavy flak guns and 272 nebelwerfer rocket launchers, though in reality much of this equipment was spread throughout the German defensive zones. The best defensive weapons in the Main Line of Resistance were just seventeen Pak 43s, the dedicated tank killer version of the 88mm flak gun, belonging to Panzerjäger Battalion 200. Just eight 88mm flak guns from Flak Battalion 305 supplemented these.

Divisional artillery was a hotchpotch of captured French and Russian guns deployed on the reverse slopes of the Bourguébus Ridge. Most of the 88mm anti-aircraft guns belonged the 3rd Flak Corps, which was under strict orders from Panzergruppe West to defend the Caen-Falaise road from air attack. Most of the guns were therefore to the south and east of Bourguébus with air defence a priority.

Panzer Mk IVs of Panzer Regiment 22 (belonging to 21st Panzer), along with the Tiger tanks, were caught in the Allied saturation bombing near Château de Manneville sixteen miles east of Caen. The effects were devastating, with tanks tossed upside-down like toys. From a force of about fifty panzers over half were lost; many others suffered mechanical problems.

The 16th Luftwaffe Field Division was incapable of withstanding the bombardment and encroaching enemy tanks, and in reality was little more than a sacrificial lamb. The 21st's Panzergrenadier Regiment 192 was at risk of being overrun and 1st Battalion Panzergrenadier Regiment 125 was cut off at le Mensil Frémental, to the east, though 2nd Battalion was holding on at Emiéville and Guillerville.

The village of le Mesnil-Fremental lay right in the middle of the British line of attack. The 21st Panzer Division's five batteries from its assault gun battalion were deployed at Démouville, Giberville, Gentheville and the farms of le Mensil-Frémental and le Prieuré, supported by von Luck's panzergrenadiers. On the eastern half of the battlefield they represented the Germans' only mobile tactical reserve.

These forces attempted to hold up the British advance, but the guns at Cuverville and Démouville were lost in the opening bombardment and the battery at Giberville withdrew northwest of Bras and, along with those at Grentheville, shelled British tanks to the east and west. The two batteries at the farms, lacking infantry protection, were also soon forced back by the relentless tide of enemy tanks. The assault gun battalion engaged the British 29th Brigade's lead regiment, the Fife and Forfar Yeomanry, destroying more than twenty Shermans before conducting a fighting withdrawal towards the 1st SS 'stop line' on Bourguébus ridge.

The British armour had 3,000 yards of open ground to cover before they reached the ridge marked by the villages of Bras, Hubert Folie and Bourgébus itself, all of which were tough German strongpoints. They got to within a few hundred yards before the Germans opened fire, knocking out four tanks in quick succession, followed by at least another seven to their right. A Squadron of the 3rd Battalion Royal Tank Regiment swiftly lost thirty-four of its fifty-two tanks.

Just after 0930, determined to hold Cagny and the vital Bourguébus, the Germans threw the 21st Panzer and 503 Heavy Panzer Battalion at the Guards and 11th Armoured Divisions with orders to regain the Caen-Troarn road. About forty-six panzers of 1st Battalion, SS Panzer Regiment 1, were thrown into action against the British in the area of the Bourguébus at 1620. Taking up positions on the Bourguébus Ridge the division inflicted heavy casualties on the British 7th and 11th Armoured Divisions, who received a very nasty surprise with the appearance of the 1st SS.

The Panthers of the 1st SS also rolled down from Bourguébus Ridge, driving back the British. In the process of trying to force them back to Caen-Troarn the two panzer divisions lost 109 tanks, while by the end of the first day the British had suffered 1,500 casualties and 200 tanks destroyed for the gain of just six miles beyond the Orne. However, the north-south line from Frénouville to Emiéville held and, with the commitment of the 1st SS Goodwood, came to a grinding halt over the next few bloody days.

Exhausted by the fighting, the panzers of 1st SS wanted to break off combat on the Bourguébus Ridge, but their request was denied due to the activity of Allied fighter-bombers; presumably on the grounds that if they stayed in close proximity to the British they were at less risk of air attack. Although German losses were high they achieved the desired effect and the 11th Armoured Division lost 106 of its tanks. West of Cagny the Guards Armoured Division was also held up, having lost sixty tanks.

Now that the Bourguébus Ridge was such a bloody killing ground, when the panzergrenadiers from 1st SS moved up on the night of 18/19 July they must have been fearful that the Allied bombers would repeat the previous day's attack. The British brought up artillery on the 19th to cover the advancing tanks, but the Northants Yeomanry veered towards Ifs to the west of Bras and were driven back toward Caen. At Bras the 1st SS defenders were not so lucky and were ejected at 1900 with the loss of a dozen self-propelled guns and many dead. By 1740 the entire 3rd Battalion, SS Panzergrenadier Regiment 1, had been destroyed in and around Bras.

Heavy rain and the actions of the 1st SS and 21st Panzer Divisions brought Goodwood to a halt on 20 July. In just two days the British 2nd Army had lost 413 tanks - some thirty-six per cent of its total tank strength. The 1st SS, 12th SS and 21st Panzer had effectively hemmed in Goodwood.

By this point, west of Bourguébus at Verrières on the far side of the Caen-Falaise road, the 1st SS had gathered seventy Panzer IVs and Panthers. A Kampfgruppe from 2nd Panzer and the 272nd Infantry Division were also on the ridge, while the 116th Panzer was in the process of moving up behind the 12th SS. It would be another month of hard fighting before the Germans were finally defeated at Falaise. In the meantime Montgomery's reputation had taken a battering.

American Sherman tanks of the US 741st Tank Battalion photographed just prior to D-Day. Note the different types of hull; the nearest tank is cast while the second is welded. Both vehicles are fitted with extended air intakes to allow for wading through the surf. The 741st Tank Battalion was to play a key role in repulsing the 12th SS Panzer Division at the Elsenborn Ridge during the Battle of the Bulge and the capture of Leipzig at the end of the war.

A Canadian Sherman coming ashore on Juno beach on 6 June 1944. The Sherman proved to be woefully inadequate during the fighting in Normandy and indeed the rest of the northwest Europe campaign. The Allies had to rely on the quantity rather than the quality of their tanks. The Canadian Army subsequently played a key role in the battle for the Scheldt Estuary.

One of the more weird and wonderful specialized armoured fighting vehicles used by the British 79th Armoured Division on D-Day. This is a Churchill AVRE Carpet Layer (Type D) Mark III. Known as the Bobbin, this was designed to lay a carpet of hessian reinforced with tubular steel scaffold tubes over patches of soft clay on the invasion beaches. The (Type C) Mark II that was also used carried a smaller diameter reel.

Two universal carriers and a Churchill AVRE passing through Lion sur Mer on 6 June 1944. The Churchill AVRE or Armoured Vehicle Royal Engineers was armed with the specially-designed 290mm Petard spigot mortar that fired a 40lb projectile containing a 26lb demolition charge known as the 'Flying Dustbin'; this had an effective range of eighty yards. They were among the first vehicles to land on the Normandy beaches and were used throughout the northwest Europe campaign to destroy enemy strongpoints.

The amphibious DUKW was also used throughout the northwest Europe campaign. Intended for a ship-to-shore role, it ended up supporting amphibious assaults across Europe's major rivers.

A British Army road sign. The Orne and Dives rivers on the Allies' eastern flank were major obstacles that had to be overcome; these were followed by the barriers created by the Seine, Scheldt and Rhine.

A British Churchill tank belonging to the 7th Royal Tank Regiment supporting infantry in the Normandy countryside. The original plan was to discontinue the Churchill, but after its sterling performance in Tunisia it was used throughout the northwest Europe campaign as an infantry support tank.

Allied bombs falling on German defences in Normandy. As can be seen from the craters peppered across the landscape, these were not pinpoint attacks. The Allies launched a series of offensives trying to surround and capture Caen. Often the bombing hampered Allied tanks as much as the panzers.

Morale looks good, but this shot was posed for the camera. Members of the Canadian 3rd Infantry Division are taking a tea break in Caen. Some of them are clearly vehicle crews, identifiable by their dusk goggles. The Canadians launched a frontal assault on the city on 7 July 1944, with Operation Charnwood taking the northern half of Caen. They then launched Operation Atlantic in conjunction with Goodwood.

The crew of a British Loyd Carrier and six-pounder anti-tank gun from the Durham Light Infantry take a closer look at a German Panther tank knocked out during Operation Epsom. This was launched on 25 June 1944 west of Caen toward Evrecy south of the city and was intended as a pre-emptive strike to tie up German panzer reinforcements. The photo was taken on 27 June at the junction of the D139 and 173a between Fontenay-le-Pesnel, Rauray and Cheux. Although the Loyd Carrier was produced by Vivian Loyd & Co. it was co-produced by other manufacturers and was used in personnel, weapons-carrying and towing roles.

British Cromwell tanks crossing 'York' Bailey pontoon bridge spanning the Caen canal and Orne river during Operation Goodwood. As well as Bailey bridges the Allies increasingly relied on specialized amphibious vehicles to support their armoured assaults across Europe's major rivers.

British Sherman tanks and a Sherman Crab flail tank, plus supporting infantry, gathered for Operation Goodwood on 18 July 1944. This British offensive east of Caen was intended to assist the capture of the city and pin down German forces prior to the American breakout from the Contentin peninsula to the west.

The Sherman Crab Mark I flail tank was instrumental in helping clear enemy minefields. Three regiments of the British 79th Armoured Division were equipped with Crabs and these operated under the 30th Armoured Brigade.

More Cromwells moving up for the attack.

The powerful Pak 43 88mm anti-tank gun. The Germans had seventeen of these available during Goodwood. Montgomery and his generals greatly underestimated the depth and strength of German defences to the east of Caen, which were anchored on the commanding high ground of the Bourguébus Ridge.

Cromwells and armoured cars of the British 7th Armoured Division. On departing from Italy the division had handed its Shermans to the Canadians and once back in Britain was reequipped with the Cromwell. This tank was really too lightly armoured to take on the panzers.

A British tank goes up in a ball of fire. The German defences on the Bourguébus Ridge effectively halted three British armoured divisions dead in their tracks. Remarkably the Allies were able to easily shrug off the loss of 400 tanks. From left to right are a Sherman Crab with its turret reversed, a Universal carrier, a Sherman gun tank and two jeeps.

The remains of a flipped German Panther tank – Goodwood was faced head on by the 1st SS, 21st and 12th SS Panzer Divisions. After initial teething problems the Panther proved a highly capable tank – this one appears to have been hit by an air attack. The bottom of the hull has clearly been penetrated in a number of places.

A Canadian Universal Carrier passes grateful French civilians. Canada built both the Universal and Windsor Carrier; some 5,000 of the latter were built during 1944-45. Following Goodwood the panzers were increasingly fighting a war of attrition that they could not win.

Camouflaged Jagdpanthers of Panzerjager Battalion 654 head for battle. Based on the Panther chassis and armed with the 88mm Pak 43 they were very few in number in Normandy, about a dozen at most. They later played a role in Hitler's surprise Ardennes offensive.

Two American breakdown trucks trying to recover a German Sturmgeschutz III assault gun. It has thrown its tracks and an armour-piercing round has gone through the hull just to the right of the gun mantle.

Once German resistance had been overcome in the Cotentin Peninsula, at Mortain, around Caen and at Falaise the next major obstacle for Allied tanks was the Seine. Pontoon bridges such as this were instrumental in crossing Europe's major rivers.

A rather blurred shot of a British Carrier about to cross a Bailey bridge. The engineers and sappers were the unsung heroes of the armoured divisions.

Looking slightly similar to the British carrier, this is an American M29 cargo carrier somewhere in Normandy. The M29C Weasel amphibious variant was to be used in the Scheldt and Rhine crossings.

Chapter Two

Rearguard at St Lambert

Following the American break out in Normandy in late July 1944 and the collapse of the tenacious German defence, a huge trap formed around Falaise. For two days the 2nd Panzer Division fought to hold open the German line of retreat at Lambert-sur-Dives in the face of the encroaching Canadian and Polish armies. Thanks to this last-ditch action the 10th SS and 116th Panzer managed to cross the Dives via the St Lambert bridge and drive the encircling Allies away; 116th Panzer escaped with fifty vehicles.

Colonel von Gersdorff, 7th Army's Chief of Staff, having lost contact with the Panzergruppe, was completely lost on the night of 19/20 August. Arriving at the southern entrance to St Lambert at around 0400 he found a column of vehicles and quickly took charge. Canadian armour and anti-tank guns were dominating the Trun-St Lambert-Chambois road, destroying anything that attempted to use it.

Gersdorff rallied two Mark V Jagdpanzers from 2nd Panzer to clear the route. Following in his Kubelwagen Gersdorff led a column of panzers, assault guns, self-propelled guns and half-tracks in a desperate bid to break through. The enemy anti-tank gunners were taken by surprise and surrendered, but the advance was held up after the lead panzers were knocked out.

In a nearby orchard Gersdorff took stock of his command and found he had a Kampfgruppe of about eight panzers, six assault guns, twenty-five to thirty armoured personnel carriers and a number of Hornisse 88mm self-propelled anti-tank guns and Hummel 150mm self-propelled artillery. There were also about 1,000 infantry from the 12th SS or 17th SS.

Inside the shrinking German corridor 2nd Panzer, with their remaining fifteen tanks, attacked toward Canadian-held St Lambert and found the bridge intact. Their commanding officer recalled: 'The crossing of the Dives bridge was particularly horrible, the bodies of the dead, horses and vehicles and other equipment having been hurled from the bridge into the river formed a gruesome tangled mass.'

The 2nd Panzer met fierce resistance in the form of enemy tank, anti-tank and infantry fire inside St Lambert. Their panzers had to renew their efforts to break out, while from midday enemy armour resumed trying to penetrate the town. The

Germans discovered an open road between Chambois and St Lambert heading northeast.

Outside the mouth of the pocket on 20 August 2nd SS Panzer Corps attempted to reach the trapped remnants of 5th Panzer Army and 7th Army. Directing the attack from its HQ at Vimoutiers the Corps launched the operation at 0400 hours. To the south of Vimoutiers two Kampfgruppen of the 2nd SS struck toward Neauphe-sur-Dive and St Lambert. The much weaker 9th SS, which had lost an entire battalion fighting the Poles, was launched along the Champeaux road toward Trun.

For the counter-attack the very last Tiger tank joined men from the 9th SS and 12th SS equipped with nothing heavier than panzerfausts holding defensive blocking positions on the Vimoutiers-Trun road. They bumped into the Polish 1st Armoured Division near Champosoult, knocking out two Shermans and forcing the rest to retreat, then they pressed on. The Kampfgruppe broke through almost to Chambois, reaching some of those trapped there.

The 2nd SS, with just twenty panzers, were unable to achieve much and the Polish 2nd Armoured Regiment halted the 9th SS. The counter-attack came to a halt before a series of hills; 258 south of Les Chameaux, 240 at Esscorches and 262 north of Goudehard. In the afternoon these were taken, but the SS could get no further. At Hill 239, north of Goudehard, the 2nd SS were counter-attacked by sixty enemy tanks and a bitter tank battle followed, while 9th SS panzergrenadiers lacking tank support got as far the heights of Les Cosniers.

In the meantime General von Schwerin's 116th Panzer Division, covering the rear of the 47th Panzer Corps during the afternoon of the 20th, got as far as Hill 168 without being molested. In St Lambert the 116th was greeted by abandoned and destroyed debris strewn everywhere. At dusk on 20 August the brave Canadian defenders in St Lambert-sur-Dives calling down artillery fire were able to destroy the gathering German forces before they could even mount their final attack.

During the close-quarter fighting for St Lambert seven panzers, forty other vehicles and twelve 88mm guns were destroyed. In the bitter two-day battle for the village the Germans suffered 300 dead, 500 wounded and 2,100 captured, including some of the officers and men from 2nd Panzer Division, who laid down their arms under the watchful eye of Canadian Sherman tanks.

Clearing a way eastward through the choked roads between 2300 and 0100 on the night of 20/21 August the survivors of the 116th Panzer Division, with about fifty combat vehicles, broke through without notable loss. The division managed to escape with eleven Panthers, four Panzer IVs, three StuGs, and two Wespe and one Hummel self-propelled gun. One group were not so fortunate; a Kampfgruppe at

Argentan found itself left behind and tried to fight its way through at Trun, but it was not successful and surrendered.

The 9th SS vainly tried to break through again on 21 August, using two massive King Tiger tanks, but these were swiftly knocked out. The Allies began to mop up the remaining Germans trapped west of the Dives and about 18,000 troops were captured. The Allies found the surrounding countryside a charnel house, the air fouled by the stench of rotting corpses, cattle and horses.

The sight of Allied fighter-bombers brings a smile to these GIs' faces. They will have been attracted by the vapour trails or the sound of an aircraft going into an attack dive. Once the panzers were in full retreat they were harried all the way back to the Seine by British Typhoons and American Mustangs and Thunderbolts. Rouen became a major bottleneck and was heavily bombed.

Have hedge will travel. This German Marder III self-propelled gun is well camouflaged against Allied air attack – this illustrates just what a threat Allied air power was to the panzers. At the start of the Normandy campaign the panzers often moved at night; by the end of it they were retreating in broad daylight.

Another camouflaged German self-propelled gun, this time a Flakpanzer 38(t) Ausf M mounting a 20mm cannon. In Normandy this was issued to the 1st SS, 2nd, 9th and Panzer Lehr Panzer Divisions. The absence of the Luftwaffe meant the panzers had to rely on mobile anti-aircraft artillery for protection.

American troops examine the remains of a blasted panzer in Normandy that appears to have been the victim of a fighter-bomber attack. This long stretch of exposed road would have been ideal for a strafing run.

More debris in Normandy, this time a Panther and Panzer Mk IV destroyed by a rocket-firing fighter-bomber. The Panther is burned out and the Panzer IV probably fell from the road trying to evade air attack. Only German industry saved Hitler's panzer divisions from collapse.

Stripped to the waist the crew of a Sherman Firefly, from the 1st Northamptonshire Yeomanry, take on board ammunition for their 17-pounder anti-tank gun just before the start of Operation Totalise on 7 August 1944. This was the British, Canadian and Polish attack along the Caen-Falaise Road, designed to capture Falaise.

A Canadian gun team prep their 6-pounder anti-tank gun for Operation Totalise. This British 57mm gun, although designed in 1939, did not go into production until November 1941. It was the first gun to have the armour piercing, discarding sabot shot, which was issued in June 1944 in time for the Normandy campaign. Another gun is just visible behind the first and their Carrier is parked to the left.

This was the fate of many Germans as they sought to escape the Falaise pocket. This unfortunate driver was shot through the windscreen and killed outright. His oak-leaf camouflage was clearly no good at hiding him from enemy gunners or aircraft.

A pilot's eye view of the battle. This farmhouse and surrounding trees proved to be no hiding place for this fleeing German armoured column. A prime mover half-track is just visible in the middle of the shot, while a truck is to the right.

A second pilot's eye view of the destruction wrought on the German Army. This German column consists of abandoned artillery, half-tracks, trucks and horses caught in the open by air attack or artillery. The vehicle on the left appears to be the Sd Kfz 250 light armoured personnel carrier.

A Humber Mk IV armoured car from the 7th Reconnaissance Regiment (17th Duke of York's Royal Canadian Hussars), which served with the Canadian 3rd Infantry Division. The British and Canadians made far greater use of armoured cars than the other armies fighting in Europe. The Humber Mk IV came into service in 1942 and had a US 37mm gun rather than the earlier 15mm Besa machine gun. The Canadians also built over 1,500 of them and dubbed it the Fox.

A Sherman Crab in action, throwing up a cloud of dirt. Reversing the turret minimised the risk of damage to the gun. Once the Germans were in retreat minefields still posed a major danger to the Allies.

A German airborne mortar team somewhere in the Bocage. German parachute troops were instrumental in helping forces trapped in the Falaise pocket to escape, and along with 2nd Panzer conducted a series of successful rearguard actions.

Clasping a souvenir German Luger pistol this Canadian soldier, photographed in St Lambert-sur-Dives, is sitting on a captured 88mm flak gun. Canadian troops bravely placed themselves directly in the way of the retreating panzers.

German soldiers surrendering to the Canadian 4th Armoured Division at St Lambert-sur-Dives, which sits in the narrow valley between the villages of Trun to the north and Chambois to the south. Montgomery ordered this remaining escape route to be closed on 17 August 1944. During the bitter two-day battle for the village the Germans lost 300 dead, 500 wounded and 2,100 captured, including officers and men from 2nd Panzer Division.

The bitter aftermath of the Falaise pocket: dead Germans lie amidst the debris. Successful German rearguard actions at St Lambert-sur-Dives and Rouen ensured that many of the panzer troops escaped to be reequipped with brand new tanks.

General Dwight D. Eisenhower taking snapshots in the Falaise pocket. Behind him is a German 105mm field gun.

Eisenhower in jovial mood touring the Normandy battlefields. At the time he had no way of knowing how many Germans had escaped eastward toward the Seine. Nor did he appreciate that his broad front strategy in Europe would make the defeat of Nazi Germany a grindingly slow task.

A spectacular shot of German prisoners both standing and lying in a Normandy holding pen. The rubbish on the ground shows how most of them simply discarded their personal kit. Following the German collapse at Falaise the Allies captured 50,000 German troops.

German PoWs being loaded on to a troop ship en route to Britain or America.

During a welcome lull in the fighting an M8 armoured car gets an axle change. Field mechanics ensured that where possible any battle damage was quickly made good.

A new piece of equipment for the British 79th Armoured Division. This is the Churchill Crocodile and was the only tank mounted flame-thrower used operationally by the British Army during the Second World War. This consisted of a Churchill VII tank with a flame nozzle replacing the hull-mounted machine gun, plus an armoured two-wheeled trailer, which contained the flame fuel. The first Crocodile unit joined the division shortly after D-Day.

Chapter Three

Tigers on the Seine

Once the Falaise gap was closed on 22 August 1944, trapping the German Army, the British 1st Corps under the command of the 1st Canadian Army pushed up the coast to Honfleur, while on its flank the Canadian 2nd Corps headed for the ancient city of Rouen and the River Seine. This was the nearest crossing point for those German troops now fleeing from Falaise and was their primary escape route.

There were five Luftwaffe field divisions manning the Atlantic Wall in the summer of 1944. General Hans Höcker's 17th Luftwaffe Field Division (LFD), deployed between Dieppe and Le Havre, played a major role in the fighting at Rouen, along with elements of SS-Brigadeführer Otto Baum's 2nd SS and General Gerhard Graf von Schwerin's 116th Panzer Divisions and General Walter Steinmüller's 331st Infantry Division.

The remnants of three panzer divisions, 2nd SS, 21st and 116th Panzer, were quickly mustered into Group Schwerin with about twenty battle-worthy tanks and assault guns. On the night of 23/24 August 21st Panzer and 2nd SS moved to reinforce the eastern flank of the 5th Panzer Army, between the Seine and the Risle, in an effort to protect the crossings near Rouen. The 21st Panzer was subordinate to 116th Panzer, while 2nd SS held blocking positions south and south-east of Elbeuf. By the evening of the 24th a makeshift defensive line had been established between Elbeuf and the Risle north of Brionne. The withdrawing 9th SS were also ordered to join Group Schwerin.

Providing this fighting screen for the retiring forces meant no rest for the shattered panzer divisions. The remains of 5th Panzer Army took command of the entire sector west of the Seine, ordering that Elbeuf, lying on a huge westward-facing loop in the river south of Rouen, should be held for as long as possible. This mission partly fell to Höcker's 17th LFD.

Field Marshal Model instructed General 'Sepp' Dietrich to counter-attack with his weak panzer divisions and thus a few below-strength panzergrenadier units and about thirty panzers were launched into a feeble attack that was swiftly halted. This was repeated on the 24th with similar results. In the meantime the exhausted German 7th Army, no longer capable of directing anything, was ordered to collect all available infantry units beyond the Seine.

Model's men did all they could to hold up the US 2nd Armored Division attempting to cross the River Avre at Verneuil. Suffering heavy casualties, the Americans then crossed upstream, swinging north toward Elbeuf. They penetrated the town on 24 August but the following morning were expelled by the tough 2nd SS. German resistance was so fierce that one American column attacking from the southeast was cut off for two desperate days and nights.

By the 25th, as the retreat got underway, 5th Panzer Army mustered barely 18,000 men, forty-two tanks and assault guns and 314 guns, essentially a single panzer division. These forces were pulled back to the Seine bridgehead formed by three large river loops to protect the crossings at Caudebec-en-Caux, Duclair, Elbeuf and Rouen. Höcker's men were assigned the high ground on the eastern bank opposite Elbeuf, blocking the crossing and the way to Rouen. Some might question the wisdom of deploying an inadequate LFD in such a key position, but it was a matter of expediency.

Some surviving Tigers of SS Heavy Panzer Battalion 102 reached Elbeuf on 25 August only to find the bridge down, so they headed for Oissel to the north-east. There the crews found the area clogged with an estimated 7,000 vehicles all waiting to cross. Reluctantly the order was given for the remaining panzers to be destroyed. Heavy Panzer Battalion 503 lost the last of its Tigers west of the Seine near Rouen at la Bouille. There were no ferries that could take their massive weight and they had to be abandoned.

Employing a combination of tanks and artillery, General Schwerin's 116th Panzer scored a minor success at Bourgtheroulde on the 26th, briefly driving the American tanks back. On the night of 26/27 August the 116th's Panzergrenadiers were deployed along the Seine loop near Moulineaux to the north and the Forêt de la Londe in the centre respectively, with 2nd SS holding the left wing near Orival, thereby blocking off the approaches to Rouen.

The 116th Panzer and a Kampfgruppe from the 2nd SS were given the task of holding the Americans at Elbeuf, but on the 26th US 2nd Armoured overran the town's southern outskirts. Having pinned down the Americans, the 116th withdrew at midnight under the cover of fog and rain; members of the 2nd SS escaped by swimming across the river. At daybreak the Americans mopped up resistance and handed the town over to the Canadians. The 10th SS crossed at Oissel on 25-27 August by means of two bridges they had seized from other German units.

A withdrawal to the three Seine loops south of Caudebec-en-Caux, south of Duclair and south of Rouen was ordered on the night of the 27/28, with the 331st

Infantry Division taking over the Duclair and Rouen loops and the dense forest in between. General Steinmüller's 331st had already gained experience of conducting rearguard actions during the escape from the Falaise pocket, and supported by elements of Panzer Lehr they remained north of Gráce defending the Gráce-Vimoutiers road.

Höcker's antiquated artillery and few anti-tank guns did what they could, enduring air attack and artillery bombardment. However, by nightfall on the 28th the Canadian 3rd and 4th Armoured Divisions had taken possession of their defensive positions on hills about a mile inland from Elbeuf, having put the 17th LFD to flight. The Polish 1st Armoured Division also crossed at Elbeuf on the 29th. In the early hours of the following day the 331st Infantry, still acting as rearguard, finally pulled back across the river and the Canadian 3rd and 4th Armoured liberated Rouen.

Tiger tank crews slipped back across the Seine on 31 August to destroy the abandoned Tigers on the Rouen dockside, as Will Fey relates:

> We pushed the explosive charges, which every panzer carried in case they were needed, into the breech of the 88mm gun, poured gasoline from a jerry can into the interior, activated the detonator charge, and threw a hand grenade into the engine compartment to set the fuel on fire.

After Falaise German armoured vehicle losses were modest considering the rapidity of the Allies' advance. Only sixty panzers and 250 other armoured vehicles were left on the west bank and about 10,000 troops were captured. In part thanks to the rearguard action at Rouen there was no second Falaise pocket. Frustratingly for the Allies, the bulk of those German forces west of the Seine, some 240,000 troops, 30,000 vehicles and 135 panzers, escaped over the river to fight another day.

GMC 6x6 amphibian DUKWs being shipped over to France. Although unarmoured, this vehicle was ideal for ferrying duties from ship to shore and across wide rivers. The later British version, the 8x8 Terrapin, was far less successful and suffered from a number of design faults.

This Landing Ship Tank is unloading new rolling stock. Much of the French railway system had been damaged during the run up to D-Day, to stop the movement of Hitler's panzer divisions. As a result the Allies had to rely on thousands of trucks to move supplies across Europe.

A German prisoner is escorted to the rear past a cast and welded hull Sherman. Arguably the most successful tank of the war, what it lacked in the design department it more than made up for in sheer numbers produced and robustness.

This burning Sd Kfz 251 armoured personnel carrier lies abandoned at the roadside. As the Germans fled toward the Seine lack of fuel forced them to leave their vehicles wherever they stopped.

American heavy artillery moving to the front. This is a 'Long Tom' M2 155mm gun. Artillery proved instrumental in breaking up panzer attacks throughout the northwest Europe campaign, especially during the Battle of the Bulge when the Germans were driven back by proximity fuses. This particular gun is fitted with a camouflage rig, probably to help protect it from enemy counter-battery fire rather than the Luftwaffe.

Another shot of the Studebaker Weasel, which had been designed early in the war for over snow operations and special missions. The first version, the M28, was superseded by the M29 in 1943, which had the engine at the front right instead of the rear.

Two grainy newspaper shots of American M10 tank destroyers and Sherman tanks crossing a pontoon bridge over the Seine. Once the Allies were over the river it became imperative that the Germans evacuate all their heavy equipment to the eastern bank.

Another US armoured column, consisting of M10s and Shermans, heading east. Following the collapse of the panzers at Falaise the Allies tried to create a larger loop as they sped toward the Seine.

A Panther Ausf G belonging to the 12th SS Panzer Division, knocked out by the Canadian Army. After the Panzer Mk IV the Panther was the most numerous German tank in Normandy.

Under new ownership. Americans with a requisitioned Kubelwagen, the German answer to the Jeep.

Canadian gunners with the huge 17-pounder anti-tank gun. This was the best anti-tank weapon the Allies possessed during much of the northwest Europe campaign. It was one of the few guns that could easily cope with the armour of the Tiger I and Tiger II.

Abandoned German armoured personnel carriers and self-propelled guns on the dockside in Rouen: visible on the right are three Marders. During the German Rückmarsch, or retreat, the Germans coaxed many of their armoured fighting vehicles back to the Seine, but the want of fuel and bridges left them unable to get them over the river. Allied bombers then did the rest by attacking the docks.

Burnt and twisted, an abandoned 88mm Flak gun and two prime mover half-tracks. Although an anti-aircraft gun, this had a dual role as an anti-tank weapon, but the dedicated Pak 43 tank killer was far more effective.

Vehicles of the Canadian 4th Armoured Division crossing a pontoon bridge over the Seine near Elbeuf on 28 August 1944. The Canadians were resisted by a hodgepodge of German units that included men from the Army, Waffen-SS and Luftwaffe.

A column of troops from the Canadian 2nd Infantry Division passing through Rouen on 31 August 1944, having put the 17th Luftwaffe Field Division and 331st Infantry Division to flight.

More abandoned equipment: this time Tiger tanks captured on a railway siding. Some panzer crews slipped back into Rouen to destroy some of the Tigers and Panthers abandoned on the dockside, to prevent them falling into enemy hands.

A military vehicle graveyard that comprises an assortment of captured carriers and motor transport. The tracked vehicle on the left is a Steyr 470 Raupenschlepper Ost that was designed for use on the Eastern Front. The small carrier on the right by the ambulance is an Infanterie Schlepper UE 630(f), originally built for the French Army and requisitioned by the Germans.

Bedraggled German prisoners under the watchful eye of US troops. Following the German rearguard action at Rouen the Allies only captured another 10,000 men, 50 panzers and 250 other armoured fighting vehicles – effectively a division's worth of enemy troops.

Following the Allied victory in Normandy a sense of optimism pervaded the Allied armies. Little did they know that the battles for Arnhem, the Scheldt, Ardennes and the Rhine would require even more bloodletting.

A symbol of defeat: a knocked out Tiger II in Normandy. Hitler was never able to deploy large numbers of these tanks during the northwest Europe campaign, though they were later to feature in his unsuccessful Ardennes offensive. Even then their performance was poor.

Chapter Four

Shermans on Hell's Highway

After the battles in Normandy Lieutenant General Wilhelm 'Willi' Bittrich found himself in the Netherlands surveying his 2nd SS Panzer Corps. It was in a poor state, having narrowly escaped the German defeat in France. Lieutenant Colonel Walter Harzer's 9th SS Panzer Division numbered only 6,000 men with just twenty Panther tanks (although it did have a large number of other armoured fighting vehicles, such as self-propelled guns, armoured cars, and forty armoured personnel carriers). Its sister division, the 10th SS under Major General Heinz Harmel, mustered barely 3,500 men and hardly any tanks. Bittrich was also able to call on elements of a heavy tank battalion equipped with Tiger tanks.

Bittrich was unaware that his command lay directly in the path of a major Allied thrust intended to 'bounce' the Rhine, turn Adolf Hitler's flank and overrun the Ruhr. Despite the developing Allied threat to the German city of Aachen, German intelligence judged that the Allies would strike toward Arnhem, which lay on the northern bank of the Dutch Rhine. By the middle of the month the 9th SS was located in a triangle formed by Arnhem-Zutphen-Apeldorn. They were scheduled to withdraw to Germany for a much-needed refit and had been ordered to hand over their vehicles to the 10th SS. The 9th SS had also despatched forces to support Kampfgruppe Walther (part of Colonel-General Kurt Student's 1st Parachute Army), which numbered twenty-five armoured vehicles including some Panther tanks and assault guns.

Allied Top Secret ULTRA signal intercepts revealed the movement of Bittrich's armoured divisions to the Nijmegen and Arnhem area, and aerial reconnaissance and the Dutch resistance also confirmed their presence. Major Tony Hibbert, British 1st Parachute Brigade, recalled a meeting with Major Brian Urquhart, chief intelligence officer, 1st Airborne Division:

> He showed me photographs of German Panzer IVs; mainly I think they were tucked in underneath woods. He went to General 'Boy' Browning

commanding the British Airborne Corps and said that in his view the operation could not succeed, because of the presence of these two divisions.

Senior British commanders would not be distracted by this inconvenient news. When Urquhart presented his findings to his boss he found himself put on sick leave. Browning, with just a week to prepare, decided that the operation would go ahead.

Montgomery, normally a cautious general, showed uncharacteristic boldness with his narrow front thrust and chose to ignore the intelligence about Bittrich's SS panzer divisions. Besides, what threat could these exhausted units pose? Operation Market Garden was simplicity itself and therein lay its flaw. 'Market', the airborne element employing four divisions of the Allied 1st Airborne Army, was to grab the bridges at Einhoven, Son and Vehgel (US 101st), Grave and Nijmegen (US 82nd) and Arnhem and Oosterbeek (British 1st plus Polish 1st Parachute Brigade), with the airlifted 52nd (Lowland) Infantry Division securing Deelem on day five. This airborne assault was to involve 34,600 airborne troops delivered by a combination of parachute and glider.

On the ground, carrying out the 'Garden' element, Lieutenant General Brian Horrocks's British 30th Corps, with the Guards Armoured Division (comprising an armoured and a mechanized infantry brigade), was to barge its way up Highway 69 (which for reasons that were soon to become apparent was to be renamed 'Hell's Highway'), followed by the 43rd Wessex and 50th Northumbrian Infantry Divisions.

The Guards Armoured Division had come ashore in Normandy in late June and had subsequently experienced a severe hammering, along with 11th Armoured, during Monty's ill-fated Operation Goodwood. Horrocks's 30th Corps was flanked by 12th and 8th Corps respectively.

In theory they were to reach Einhoven on day one, Nijmegen on the second day and Arnhem by day four. General Horrocks was not altogether happy about the plan

> The country was wooded and rather marshy which made any flanking operation impossible. The only thing I could do was blast my way down the main road on a comparatively narrow front with as much air and artillery support as I could get.

British 1st Airborne would end up on its own for ten gruelling days thanks to Bittrich's efforts.

Just four days before Market Garden kicked off, General Browning issued the following assessment:

The total armoured strength is probably not more than 50-100 tanks …

> There is every sign of the enemy strengthening the river and canal lines through Nijmegen and Arnhem … but the troops manning them are not numerous and many are of low category.

There is no disputing that Market Garden was a potentially decisive plan intended to capitalize on the Germans' apparent disarray. In particular the 1st Airborne Division had been held back on D-Day and was now chomping at the bit to have a go. Unfortunately, the bulk of 1st Airborne landed around Arnhem by 1400 on 17 September 1944 in complete ignorance of the presence of the SS armour.

Bittrich and his 2nd SS Panzer Corps learned of the British airborne drop five minutes after it started. He immediately called for the bridges at Nijmegen and Arnhem to be brought down to stop them falling into enemy hands, but Field Marshal Model refused, claiming that they would be needed for the counter-attack. Following some initial confusion Bittrich's two divisions quickly cobbled together various Kampfgruppen, or battle groups.

The US 101st Airborne achieved the majority of its objectives by 1600 on the 17th with 501st Parachute Infantry Regiment securing the road and rail bridges at Heeswijk and Veghel, 502nd PIR the St Oedenrode bridge, though at Son the road bridge was brought down before the 506th PIR could secure it and at another bridge south of Best they were turned back. The 82nd's 508th and 505th Parachute Infantry established defensive positions either side of Groesbeek village, while the 504th took Grave Bridge. Unfortunately, two of the three bridges over the Maas-Waal Canal were blown. American paratroopers were sent into Nijmegen to reconnoitre the bridge across the River Waal, but were halted in their tracks by Kampfgruppe Henke.

At 1400 on 17 September, 408 guns of General Horrocks's 30th Corps opened fire to support the initial advance of the Irish Guards battle group on a two-tank-wide front with infantry from the 231st Brigade from 50th (Northumbrian) Division. The 12th Corps under Lieutenant General N.M. Ritchie attacked north, with the 15th (Scottish) Division and 53rd (Welsh) Division striking the Germans' Kampfgruppe Chill.

Horrocks's opening breakthrough went well, with dazed Kampfgruppe Walther being unable withstand the blasting it received. 'To start with everything seemed to be going our way,' recalled General Horrocks. 'But suddenly nine of the Irish Guards' tanks were knocked out almost all at once and a furious battle began in the woods in front of me.'

The Guards' tanks broke out of their Meuse-Escaut canal bridgehead and rolled into the Netherlands at 1500. They then ran into elements of two battalions of the 9th SS and two German parachute battalions. These were pushed aside, but crucially

30th Corps only covered half the anticipated distance. By 1930 the Guards Armoured Division was stalled at Valkenswaard.

The 9th SS, although preparing to transit home, quickly sent its reconnaissance battalion south over the Arnhem highway bridge toward Nijmegen. Another battle group sped westward toward Oosterbeek, where most of 1st Airborne was located: this would prevent reinforcements reaching those British paratroops already in Arnhem. To avoid losing them Harzer had removed the tracks and wheels from some of his vehicles and deliberately reported them unserviceable, so it was not until late afternoon that sufficient numbers of tanks were battle-ready.

The following day, the 9th SS reconnaissance battalion, leaving a few self-propelled guns to guard the southern approaches of Nijmegen bridge, headed north to Elst. A column of twenty-two vehicles then attempted to force a crossing of Arnhem bridge, the northern end of which was by now firmly in British hands. Half the vehicles were destroyed and the SS were driven off amidst a blaze of gun fire.

The 10th SS was despatched to Nijmegen to hold the main bridges against the Guards' advancing armour: this was key to isolating and destroying the paratroops at Oosterbeek west of Arnhem. However, with Arnhem bridge in British hands the bulk of the 10th SS was obliged to use the ferry at Pannerden eight miles (13km) south-east of Arnhem. Twelve Panthers reached the Nijmegen area and Arnhem bridge was finally secured on 20 September.

'It was 1100 hours on the morning of Thursday 21 September,' according to Geoffrey Powell, a company commander with 4 Para Brigade, 'before the Irish Guards received orders to break through to Arnhem Bridge … Waiting for them were German infantry, by now well dug-in and supported by tanks and SP guns.' Unfortunately they did not move off until 1230 (nineteen hours after the capture of Nijmegen road bridge) and within twenty minutes had lost three tanks blocking the highway.

'For three days now,' recalled Powell, 'the dogged resistance of brigadeführer Harmel's SS troops, fighting in the Betuwe between Nijmegen and Arnhem, had slowed the pace of the British advance.' To the south the Panthers of Kampfgruppe Walther attacked toward Veghel, between Eindhoven and Nijmegen, on the 22nd. The 9th SS, reinforced by Heavy Panzer Battalion 506, consisting of some sixty powerful King Tigers, set about eliminating the defenders at Oosterbeek. Luckily for the paras these attacks were not very well coordinated.

The 10th SS were eventually forced back, so Bittrich sent forty-five Tigers and a company of Panthers to reinforce them, following the landing of the Polish 1st Parachute Brigade at Driel south of Oosterbeek. Geoffrey Powell recalled: 'defeated at Nijmegen, the 10th SS Panzer Division had retired towards Arnhem and was now waiting for 30th Corps' next move.'

The continually delayed British tanks struggling north along the single exposed road, under constant counter-attack, could simply not get through and on 26 September the decision was taken to evacuate the exhausted paratroops trapped at Oosterbeek. The SS had lost 3,300 casualties, including 1,100 dead in the fighting. The British 1st Airborne Division at the start of the operation numbered just over 10,000: only 2,163 escaped back across the Rhine, leaving 1,485 dead and 6,414 captured.

While the Allies managed to seize eight of the crossings, the failure to secure the ninth at Arnhem, thanks to the presence of Bittrich's panzers, meant the failure of Montgomery's laudable plan. His fundamental objective had been to force the Maas and Rhine in one bound, but the presence of the SS ensured that he failed. Total Allied losses for the operation were in excess of 17,000, while the Germans lost up to10,000 troops.

Montgomery's plan for Operation Market Garden, whilst uncharacteristically bold, was over ambitious – in part it relied on two recuperating SS panzer divisions being unfit to fight. All attempts to flag up the threat posed by these recuperating panzers by the Dutch underground and British intelligence were ignored, with dire consequences.

Lieutenant General Brian Horrocks, commander of 30th Corps. It was the task of his armour from the Irish Guards Group (comprising infantry and tanks) to cut their way to the bridge over the Rhine at Arnhem. If this could be achieved the Allies could hook left into the Nazis' industrial heartland in the Ruhr and overrun Hitler's weapons factories.

Taking the bridges at Nijmegen and Arnhem was key to the whole success of Operation Market Garden. The quick reactions of the 9th SS and 10th SS Panzer Divisions fatally slowed the Allied push north, leaving the British paras trapped.

British and American medics unloading German wounded from a requisitioned Sd Kfz 251 armoured half-track. By September 1944 the German armed forces were in a state of disarray and the Allies hoped to take advantage of this situation to hasten the end of the war.

Americans examine a knocked out Panther. Judging by the damage to the hull its ammunition exploded, ripping out the side and buckling the road wheels. Such a blast would have incinerated the crew. In early September 1944 Army Group B could muster just 100 combat-ready panzers. On paper it seemed that nothing could stop the Guards' thrust to Arnhem.

A British Sherman crew fraternise with Dutch locals just prior to the Arnhem attack. The Guards Armoured Division were given the task of forcing their way up the exposed and narrow Highway 69. The quick reaction of various German battle groups along the route was to ensure that this was a painfully slow process.

Another British tank photographed just prior to Market Garden, this time a Cromwell with its turret festooned in netting and equipment. This was numerically the most important British-built cruiser tank of the Second World War, forming the main tank force of the British armoured divisions in 1944-45, along with the American supplied M4 Sherman. However, by 1944, even with a 75mm gun, it was inferior to the Panther and Panzer Mk IV.

An interesting shot of British Shermans, carriers and jeeps waiting for the jump-off. The column clearly includes a press-ganged German Sd Kfz 251 armoured personnel carrier. The Irish Guards Group was preceded by a barrage of 350 guns, intended to blast a path for it.

The lightly-armed British 1st Airborne Division landed in the Arnhem area on 17 September 1944 ignorant of the presence of the 2nd SS Panzer Corps. The man on the left is equipped with a PIAT anti-tank weapon. 1st Airborne ended up fighting on its own for ten gruelling days against the panzers.

German prisoners from the 9th SS Panzer Division captured at Arnhem. These men came from the division's reconnaissance battalion. Their presence was an unpleasant surprise for the British 1st Airborne.

Traffic jams were inevitable. 'It looked as though we should have to advance on one road only,' said General Horrocks, 'and in the corps were 20,000 vehicles.' It was imperative that Highway 69 be kept open so vehicles knocked out or disabled were swiftly shunted out of the way. Here Shermans of the Irish Guards pass tanks that were hit earlier by the German defences. The nearest Sherman has clearly caught fire. It became dubbed 'Hell's Highway' for good reason.

German prisoners being escorted to the rear by three carriers belonging to the 53rd (Welsh) Infantry Division. This formed part of the left-flanking British 12th Corps. On the night of 17/18 September 1944 the division attacked across the Escaut Canal near Lommel taking on German paratroops.

Paratroops from the US 101st Airborne Division hitch a ride on a British Cromwell tank ready to take the rail and road bridges at Nijmegen. They had to overcome 500 very determined Germans dug in at Valkhof and Hunner Park at the southern end of the highway bridge.

A Guards armoured car is mobbed by curious Dutch civilians in Grave, southwest of Nijmegen, after the British linked up with the US 82nd Airborne Division.

A series of shots showing the Guards Armoured Division crossing the Nijmegen road bridge near the Valkhof. In the first image are Cromwell tanks and a carrier; the second shows Sexton self-propelled guns and the third is of a column of Shermans being led by a Sherman Firefly. German attempts to demolish both bridges and stop the tanks failed. In case the Germans brought down any of the bridges a huge amount of bridging material was assembled, along with 9,000 sappers and 2,300 vehicles.

A blown up British carrier. The width of the British corridor did not allow manoeuvrability and the fringes were mined in many places.

An abandoned Jadgpanther somewhere in the Netherlands. The Germans proved very adept at cobbling together units for instant counter-attacks.

British infantry marching past an 88mm Flak gun, which was also capable of being used in an anti-tank role. It is unclear why it was abandoned at the roadside, but the elevation of the barrel would indicate it was being used for air defence.

Dutch civilians show their gratitude by bringing an Irish Guards tank crew food in the shape of some welcome apples. Despite 30th Corps' efforts it simply could not reach Arnhem.

A devastated Nijmegen and the bridge over the Waal, photographed on 28 September 1944. Although the Allies' seizure of this bridge was a triumph, it was simply not enough and Arnhem became, infamously, 'a bridge too far.' The weak SS panzer units stopped the British paras from holding Arnhem bridge and slowed up the armoured Guards.

Once the British were overwhelmed in Arnhem eviction from Oosterbeek could not be avoided.

Grateful British paras
hitch a lift on a
Churchill tank.

Vehicles from the 49th
(West Riding) Infantry
Division, whose
divisional sign was a
polar bear. They took
part in the Liberation
of Arnhem, which
finally happened in
mid-April 1945.

A Sherman Crab in Arnhem on 14 April 1945.

A Humber Scout car moving through the streets of Arnhem, also photographed on 14 April 1945.

Chapter Five

Buffaloes in the Scheldt

To stop the Allied push across the Netherlands and Belgium were 80,000 men of General Gustav-Adolf van Zangen's 15th Army and 18,000 men of General Student's 1st Parachute Army. Both lacked panzers. After the German defeat in Normandy the 15th Army, which had been deployed north of the Seine to deter an invasion across the Pas de Calais, had withdrawn largely intact into the Netherlands. Its new task was to deny the port of Antwerp to the Allies. Although the British 11th Armoured Division liberated the city on 4 September 1944, the Germans remained firmly dug in along the vital Scheldt Estuary to the west.

Once the British were in Antwerp the 15th Army fell back to a fortified bridgehead at the mouth of the Scheldt estuary, thereby blocking the approach to the port. It would take the Allies almost two months of heavy fighting to secure it and the Scheldt, and in the meantime much-needed supplies had to rumble across Europe from the French ports by truck. While the armour of the British 2nd Army was preparing itself for Operation Market Garden, the Canadian 1st Army was given the task of driving the Germans from the estuary.

The Canadian 4th Armoured Division was instructed to clear the south shore around the Breskens pocket and drove along the Ghent-Terneuzen Canal on 21 September. The Polish 1st Armoured Division struck north of Antwerp and along the Dutch-Belgian border. The Canadian tanks had to fight their way over the Ghent, Leopold and Schipdonk canals, suffering heavy casualties. The Poles succeeded in taking Terneuzen and clearing the south bank of the Scheldt east toward Antwerp.

Following the failure of Market Garden, opening the Scheldt to Allied shipping became a priority. The Canadians focused on the neck of the South Beveland peninsula. Their 4th Armoured Division attacked north of the Leopold Canal and captured Bergen-op-Zoom; this was followed by fighting to reduce the Breskens pocket, advance down the South Beveland peninsula and secure the island of Walcheren. Amphibious landings were carried out in two parts on 1 November and five days later the island's capital Middleburg was taken. German resistance ended on 8 November.

The defensive obstacles presented by northern Europe's rivers meant that by late 1944 the British Army was integrating increasing numbers of new amphibious vehicles. Up to that point the American Landing Vehicle Tracked (LVT) or Water Buffalo had mainly been employed in the island-hopping campaigns in the Pacific against the Japanese, but coming into service in northwest Europe it saw action during the bitter fighting to clear the Scheldt estuary. The LVT had evolved from a vehicle designed for emergency relief work in the Florida Everglades following the regular hurricanes in the mid-1930s. Designed by Donald Roebling, a militarized version was produced in 1940 for the US Marine Corps, known as the LVT1, which was followed two years later by the LVT2. The third variant was designed with a rear-loading ramp and the LVT finally came into its own as a military cargo carrier.

Armoured cargo and support variants were also produced in the shape of the LVT(A)1 and LVT(A)2, while the LVT(A)4 included the M8 Motor carriage turret armed with a 75mm howitzer. It was propelled through the water by its tracks at a speed of just seven and a half miles an hour. Due to the large track grousers, which were in a 'W' shape to provide propulsion, the vehicle could not drive on hard surfaces for any length of time before causing damage, so the LVT was unable to stray far from water. This meant that the Buffalo was usually moved on a trailer towed by the Diamond T tractor. During the war over 18,600 were built by the USA.

Those supplied to the British Army were classified as Amphibian Tracked and were used in Northern Italy, on the Scheldt and along with American ones on the Rhine. They were issued to the Royal Engineers and the Royal Tank Regiment. Most were the LVT2 and LVT(A)2, designated the Buffalo II, and the LVT4, designated the Buffalo IV. The standard armament of the Buffalo had two .30 inch machine guns at the sides, with a .50 machine gun over the driving compartment. On the Mark II the side machine guns were carried on a rail around the hold, while on the Mark IV they were pintle-mounted. However, on most British Mark IIs the rails were removed and the guns fitted to sockets midway along the hold; likewise the .50 calibres were usually replaced with a 20mm Polsten cannon. British Mk II Buffaloes were also converted to carry the 17-pounder anti-tank gun.

In the water many British crews found the Buffalo a dreadful beast. Not only was it slow, but rather than ride the waves it simply ploughed through them. In choppy seas it took on a lot of water. You had to be very careful when driving from the ramp as the Buffalo could flounder and sink. A number of crewmen were lost in this manner during training.

During the Scheldt battles 100 Buffaloes striking from Terneuzen helped ensure the south bank was cleared of Germans after an attack turned their eastern flank on 8 October 1944. Working west from Antwerp the Canadian 2nd Corps started to clear the north bank, but ran into difficulty on South Beveland. In response 174 Buffaloes carrying an assault force from the 52nd Lowland Division, supported by a squadron of DD tanks on 24 October, crossed the Scheldt. Buffaloes were then involved in the capture of Walcheren Island that dominated the mouth of the estuary. In particular 102 Buffaloes were used to attack Westkapelle on the western end of the island. The town of Middleburg was seized by a Buffalo force from the 11th Battalion Royal Tank Regiment.

The Sherman DD tanks had already proved their worth supporting British Canadian and American assault forces during D-Day on 6 June 1944, though they did have a nasty habit of capsizing in rough water. The DD tank was designed by Nicholas Straussler, who found waterproofing the hull and raising the freeboard could make a tank float without cumbersome buoyancy aids. This was done by erecting a canvas screen round the hull and was initially produced as a Valentine conversion in 1943-44, a few of them seeing service in Italy. Duplex drive – propeller and tracks – was applied to the ubiquitous M4 Sherman tank, though it could only manage 6 mph. Its low silhouette in the water enabled an element of tactical surprise on D-Day.

Similarly, the amphibious 6x6 DUKW was a veteran of the campaigns in the Mediterranean and on D-Day. The prototype was built around the cab-over-engine six-wheel-drive GMC military truck with the addition of a watertight hull and a propeller. It was not an armoured vehicle and at 7.5 tons managed just 6.4mph in water or a respectable 50-55mph on land. The DUKW rode the waves well and its bilge pumps meant it could be kept free of water. For ship to shore stores ferrying it was ideal. More than 21,000 DUKWs were manufactured, with large numbers supplied to the British Army. In the DD tank regiments the 3-ton trucks were replaced with eighteen DUKWs and eleven M29C Weasels.

In contrast, the British-built Terrapin, intended as a possible DUKW stand-in, was poorly designed in terms of storage and visibility. Also, its lack of rear loading ramp restricted its operational usefulness. One member of the 199th General Transport Company, Royal Army Service Corps (RASC) recalled that it was slow and cumbersome on both the water and land, with the steering lever making it very difficult to handle. In addition, if one of the two V8 Ford engines broke down the Terrapin was left going round in circles with no way of getting back to the shore without help.

Although 500 Terrapins were ordered in 1943 and equipped the 1st Assault Brigade of the Royal Engineers, their only notable operational use was during the Scheldt operations. The Terrapin first went into action following the attack from

Terneuzen, when forty were used to carry stores after most of the Buffaloes had broken down. During the South Beveland attack the follow-up force consisted of Buffaloes and twenty-seven Terrapins. Perhaps not surprisingly, the improved Terrapin Mk II and the British LVT equivalents Argosy and Neptune never went into production.

Likewise, the American M29C Water Weasel's main claim to fame in northwest Europe was during the operations in the Scheldt. At the end of April 1944 the US Army Engineer Board summarized:

> From the results of the investigation and test of the M29C Cargo Carrier to determine its suitability for Engineer use, it is concluded that this special purpose amphibious vehicle has high cross country mobility and is particularly suited for operation over swampy, muddy, and extremely rough terrain for crossing small bodies of calm water; it is suitable for the same general applications in swamp, jungle, or rough terrain for which the 1/4-ton, 4x4 truck or the 3/4-ton weapons carrier is used under average conditions…

Studebaker built around 15,000 M29 and M29C Weasels.

Issued to the British Army under lend-lease in late 1944, the Weasel formed part of the establishment of those regiments equipped with Buffaloes. For the attack on Walcheren a whole platoon of the 259th General Transport Company, RASC, operated Weasels, supporting the 52nd Lowland Division. Nearly seventy M29Cs were used in the assault on Walcheren on 1 November 1944.

A very good shot of Churchill Mk VI or VII tanks (the square escape hatch indicates that it is a VI) armed with 75mm guns (which replaced the earlier 6-pounder guns), somewhere in the Netherlands. The failure of Market Garden meant securing the approaches to Antwerp became a priority.

The crew of a British 79th Armoured Division Sherman, with the call sign 'Bramble 5', seem to be a source of some fascination for these Dutch villagers. This division played a key role in the Scheldt operations and the same tank was photographed on Walcheren in November 1944, with the crew replenishing their ammunition from a Buffalo Landing Vehicle Tracked.

A knocked-out Sturmgeschutz IV. By this stage of the war the German 15th Army relied almost entirely on assault gun battalions, having been stripped of all its panzer formations. This particular type of assault gun went into production in late 1943 and by the end of the war just over 1,100 had been built, having been superseded by the Jagdpanzer IV and Panzer IV/70.

German Fallschirmjäger, or paratroops, fought during 1944-45 as infantry. General Student's 1st Parachute Army, along with the 15th Army, had the job of defending the Netherlands and Belgium.

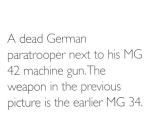

A dead German paratrooper next to his MG 42 machine gun. The weapon in the previous picture is the earlier MG 34.

DD swimming tanks such as this played a key role in the Scheldt battles. Utilising the ubiquitous M4 Sherman tank, it could only manage 6mph and the low silhouette in the water enabled an element of tactical surprise. Crews felt safer than they did on D-Day as they were less likely to drown.

A Crocodile in action displaying its fearsome flamethrower. This was an invaluable infantry support weapon used to saturate enemy strongpoints. The second unit equipped with this tank flamethrower was the 1st Fife and Forfar Yeomanry, who joined the 79th Armoured Division in early October 1944 in time to help clear S'Hertogenbosch in the southern Netherlands. Being on the receiving end of such a weapon must have been a terrifying experience, assuming that you avoided being burned alive.

The Terrapin Mk I was the unsatisfactory British equivalent of the American DUKW. Initially it was intended for a ship-to-shore role, but ended up being used as a ferry vehicle across the waterways of the Netherlands in support of amphibious operations. Design faults ensured that a Mk II was never built.

Another Terrapin of the 79th Armoured Division. They were first used to ferry the Canadian 8th Infantry Brigade across the Braakman inlet, a channel off the Scheldt, on 10 October 1944. They then took part in the amphibious assault on South Beveland on 26 October. Like many British wartime vehicles it was a rushed job and not completely thought through.

The Landing Vehicle Tracked, or LVT, was first used in support of the US Marines in the Pacific (seen here) and was then supplied to northwest Europe for use in the Scheldt and Rhine operations. The British 79th Armoured Division was equipped with the LVT 2 and the LVT 4, designated the Mk II and Mk IV respectively by the British Army.

Buffaloes taking Canadian troops across the Scheldt. As the vehicle was powered through the water by its tracks, the track design meant it could not venture very far inland before damaging them.

A column of Buffaloes passing Terrapins on the Scheldt near Terneuzen on 13 October 1944. The combination of these, DD tanks, Weasels and DUKWs proved highly successful.

Sappers of the Canadian 3rd Infantry Division preparing to sweep for mines along the border between Belgium and the Netherlands on 16 October 1944. Anti-personnel and anti-tank mines were a constant threat and could easily catch the unwary.

A very British beast. This Buffalo Mark IV, named 'Sevenoaks', is shown manoeuvring for position just before the assault on Beveland in late October 1944. It is armed with a Polsten 20mm cannon and two .30 calibre machine guns. The Polsten provided greater firepower shorewards than the standard .50 machine gun when taking part in a beach assault, and could be used for anti-aircraft defence at the same time.

M4 Sherman and M5 Stuart tanks (identifiable from the earlier M3 by the stepped rear engine deck), as well as a Humber scout car and jeeps, in Bergen-op-Zoom town square in the Netherlands on 31 October 1944.

The LVT(A)4 with its rather formidable looking 75mm howitzer. This replaced the 37mm turret on the LVT(A)1. River assault forces could pack a punch.

A destroyed German assault gun somewhere in the Netherlands. This looks to be a late model Stu H42 without muzzle break, which was armed with a 105mm howitzer designed to provide additional fire support for the Sturmgeschütz detachments.

A column of four LVT 1s whitewashed ready for winter operations. The large W-shaped track grousers that provided propulsion in the water are clearly visible; these meant that the vehicle could not be driven on roads and had to be transported on low-loaders to the point of operation.

This LCT is offloading both Buffaloes and Weasels whilst under enemy fire at Westkappelle, Walcheren Island, during the landings on 1 November 1944.

Another Buffalo swimming ashore from its LCT at Walcheren. Again the 20mm Polston cannon is visible on the front of the hull.

Soaked British Commandos struggle toward the cover of a Buffalo on Walcheren beach.

A snow-camouflaged Buffalo Mk II of 80 Assault Squadron RE during the attack on Kapelsche Veere on the south bank of the Mass. The desolate landscape looks bitterly cold.

A Buffalo Mk II conducting Rhine-crossing rehearsals embarks men of the 15th Scottish Division. Note the foot rails for quick exit and the tyre bumpers.

A Crocodile flamethrower supporting the Rifles Brigade during the attack on Sin Joost in the Netherlands. The village was destroyed during operation Blackcock, conducted by the 7th Armoured Division and two supporting infantry divisions on 20 January 1945.

Chapter Six

Panzers on the Elsenborn

Hitler's surprise winter offensive commenced on 16 December 1944 under the cover of heavy cloud and snow that kept the enemy fighter-bombers at bay. The 1st SS and 12th SS Panzer divisions launched the 6th SS Panzer Army's main thrusts. Their spearhead, formed by Kampfgruppe Peiper drawn from 1st SS, consisted of 100 Panzer Mk IV and Panthers, about forty formidable Tiger IIs and twenty-five assault guns. In addition Otto Skorzeny's Panzer Brigade 150's three Kampfgruppen were also assigned to the 1st SS and 12th SS Panzer and the 12th Volksgrenadier Division.

Directly in the line of the 12th SS Panzers' northern attack was the Elsenborn ridge. It was here that the Germans were halted dead in their tracks by the US Army and the panzers singularly failed to contribute to the huge bulge cut into the Allied lines further south. The defending US 99th Infantry Division were well dug in and their artillery and anti-tank guns played havoc with the German advance. It also forced Kampfgruppe Peiper further south, and south-east of Elsenborn the 1st SS Panzer Division was held up. Key amongst the American anti-tank units were elements of the 612th Tank Destroyer Battalion equipped with towed 3-inch guns around Höfen.

Alarm was caused when a reconnaissance tank company from Kampfgruppe Peiper's spearhead threatened Wirtzfeld on 17 December. Occupation of Wirtzfeld and the twin villages of Krinkelt-Rocherath would roll up the 2nd and 99th Infantry Divisions from the flank. If Peiper reached Bütgenbach and moved north to Elsenborn the two divisions would be caught in the rear, completely unhinging the American defences and trapping up to 30,000 men.

With the panzers making for Bullingen the Americans set up an improvized defence south of Wirtzfeld with clerks, cooks, drivers and military police. They were reinforced by divisional artillery under Brigadier-General John H. Hinds, who deployed a battery of 105mm field guns and another of heavy 155mm howitzers to cover the approaches to Wirtzfeld and Bullingen. The defenders also had some 57mm anti-tank guns and four half-tracks with quad .50 calibre machine guns.

Panzers and armoured half-tracks roared out of the mist on the Bullingen road at about 0800 hours on 17 December and crossed a ridge outside Wirtzfeld to be met by a hail of fire. At this point the Americans received welcome reinforcements in the shape of five self-propelled tank destroyers from the 644th Tank Destroyer Battalion. They destroyed four enemy vehicles in quick succession and the others withdrew to Bullingen.

Near Krinkelt-Rocherath the 12th Volksgrenadiers, supported by 12th SS tanks, set about the 99th Infantry. Even in the face of five Tigers the Americans fell back grudgingly on the twin villages. In front of Rocherath the ground was littered with German dead and seventeen tanks. The streets of Krinkelt-Rocherath became a killing ground for the panzers, where they were caught by bazooka teams and hidden tanks and tank destroyers. American artillery and mines also took a toll, often leaving panzers disabled and at the mercy of bazookas. Remarkably two Shermans claimed five Tigers in Rocherath after the Germans became trapped on the narrow streets.

Nonetheless, tanks of the US 741st Tank Battalion covering the American withdrawal were destroyed by the advancing Panthers. Desperate to drive the Americans from Elsenborn the Germans threw themselves at Höfen and Monschau only to be stopped by US artillery fire. They renewed their attacks on the twin villages on 18 December, supported by Jagdpanthers of the 560th Heavy Anti-Tank Battalion. Armed with the 88mm gun they seemed unstoppable. However, Shermans from the 741st Tank Battalion as well as artillery and bazooka fire ensured the panzers did not break free to the open ridgeline. In the meantime two US infantry divisions moved to reinforce the defenders, who withdrew to the ridge.

Switching their emphasis, the 12th SS, supported by the 12th Volksgrenadier Division, attacked Domäne Butgenbach on the southern end of the ridge on 19 December. Two days later the 12th SS were halted by M36 tank destroyers of the 613th Tank Destroyer Battalion. The last German attack on the right took place on 22 December and was greeted by a devastating 10,000 rounds fired by US artillery.

Cole Barnard, a rifleman with the US 11th Armored Division, deployed south-west of Bastogne, recalled:

There are some interesting aspects to the attack and one of them was that Hitler had created a special brigade which would go along with the lead elements of the attack, get behind our lines, and capture the Meuse River bridges so they could hold those until the rest of the troops got up there. This brigade was outfitted with all captured American and British tanks. They had all captured American weapons and were all dressed in American uniforms.

Under Operation Grief Otto Skorzeny had been personally appointed by Hitler to command Panzer Brigade 150, tasked with capturing the vital Meuse bridges at Amay, Andenne or Huy before they could be demolished. Skorzeny was summoned to Hitler's Rastenburg HQ on 22 October 1944, where he was congratulated on the success of his mission to Hungary and promoted from major to lieutenant-colonel. The Hungarian operation had used several hundred commandos from the 500th SS Parachute Battalion and the Jagdverbande. Skorzeny's coup in Budapest, though, had hardly been subtle, as a company of massive Tiger II tanks had backed his seizure of Hungarian leader Admiral Horthy.

'Stay awhile,' said Hitler. 'I am now going to give you the most important job of your life. In December Germany will start a great offensive. It may decide her fate.' He outlined Operation *Herbstnebel* (Autumn Mist) or *Wacht am Rhein* (Watch on the Rhine), the forthcoming Ardennes counter-offensive. 'He told me about the tremendous quantity of materiel which had been accumulated,' noted Skorzeny 'and I recall that he stated we would have 6,000 artillery pieces in the Ardennes, and, in addition, the Luftwaffe would have about 2,000 planes, including many of the new jet planes. He then told me that I would lead a panzer brigade which would be trained to reach the Meuse bridges and capture them intact.'

Despite Skorzeny's repeated complaints, he found himself being supplied with German equipment rather than American. Skorzeny grumbled that 'he had to make up the difference with German vehicles. The only common feature of these vehicles was that they were all painted green, like American military vehicles.' Initially his unit was equipped with five Panther tanks, five Sturmgeschütz or StuG assault guns, six German armoured cars and six armoured personnel carriers.

Skorzeny's brigade was supposed to include two companies of panzers and by late November had been supplied with twenty-two Panther tanks and fourteen StuG assault guns, with the tank crews provided by the 6th Panzer Division. Panzerjäger crews for the StuGs came from Heavy Panzerjäger Battalion 655 and the armoured car crews came from the reconnaissance battalions of the 2nd Panzer Division and 90th Panzergrenadier Division. When they finally went into battle they seem to have deployed only ten Panthers and five StuGs.

There was simply no way to make a Panther look like a Sherman, so Skorzeny's men ingeniously opted to make them look like the Sherman's tank destroyer cousin, the M10 Wolverine, based on a Sherman chassis but with a much more angular hull and turret. To do this the Panthers were disguised with sheet metal, painted olive green and given prominent white five-pointed American recognition stars. These, Skorzeny cynically noted, were only sufficient to: 'deceive very young American troops seeing them at night from very far away.'

Once Hohes Venn was reached Skorzeny's three Kampfgruppen were to pass round their assigned units, but things did not run smoothly and they got horribly tangled up at Losheim. Skorzeny realised by the evening of the second day of the offensive that Panzer Brigade 150 would simply not reach the Meuse bridges, so he suggested that his unit serve as a regular combat force. Under the direction of Colonel Wilhelm Mohnke he was ordered to help take Malmédy to open up the roads to reach Kampfgruppe Peiper.

Although the Germans destroyed 300 American tanks, Eisenhower countered Hitler's offensive by moving the US 7th Armored Division to St Vith and elements of the 10th Armored and US 101st Airborne Divisions to Bastogne. The Panzer Lehr Division was not quick enough and the GIs beat them to the town. Although the 116th Panzer Division slipped between Bastogne and St Vith, Bastogne's defenders held up 2nd Panzer. St Vith fell on 21 December, but heavy American artillery fire forced the two Panzer armies to become ever more entangled.

All three of Skorzeny's battlegroups joined 1st SS Panzer and were thrown into the attack on Malmédy on the 21st. However, any chance of his Kampfgruppen achieving a level of surprise was lost after one of his men was captured the day before and spilled the beans. To make matters worse, Skorzeny's planned attack lacked artillery support to soften up the defenders or conduct counter-battery fire when the American artillery inevitably retaliated. Luftwaffe fighter cover was also completely out of the question.

Predictably, Hauptmann Scherff and Kampfgruppe Y were met by such heavy shelling that he quickly broke off his assault. This was not the covert operation he had planned and trained for. On the left Willi Hardieck's Kampfgruppe X attacked with two companies of infantry supported by five fake M10 tank destroyers. They pushed from Ligneuville, through Bellevaux and along the route de Falize, striking west of Malmédy. The main force headed toward the Warche River bridge and Rollbahn C. Trip-wire flares illuminating the early morning gloom quickly alerted the American defenders and the fake M10s ran into a minefield and the 823rd Tank Destroyer Battalion command post, which was quickly surrounded and attacked.

Skorzeny watched from the hill on the route de Falise as one of his fake M10s, supported by German infantry in attack toward Malmédy, was driven off by an American anti-tank gun. The other nine tanks attempted to capture a bridge over the Warche in order to reach Stavelot, but the first tank was lost to a mine and began to burn. American infantry manning a roadblock were forced back, but when the Germans attempted to cross the bridge GIs armed with bazookas knocked out two more tanks. Two American tank destroyers then accounted for two further German tanks.

Skorzeny, seeing how things were progressing, ordered his men to fall back, but none of his remaining armour made it. One fake M10 coded B5 was disabled at Malmédy, another, B10, crashed into the café at La Falise. B7 got as far as the

Ambléve Bridge at Malmédy but was brought to a halt by US bazooka fire. Several Sturmgeschütz in American markings were knocked out at Géromont.

A knocked-out snow-covered Sherman, belonging to the 5th Parachute Jäger Division, photographed outside the Hotel des Ardennes, epitomized the failure of Hitler's Operation Grief. Skorzeny's fake Shermans had got him nowhere. 2nd Panzer got closer to the Meuse than special Panzer Brigade 150 ever did.

The crew of an M3A1 half-track from the US 14th Armored Division attend to a burning Sherman M4A3(76)W in Barr, Alsace, in north-eastern France, on 29 November 1944. Judging by the damage the tank took a direct hit in the rear. The US 14th Armoured, nicknamed the 'Liberators', were to cross the Rhine near Worms on 1 January 1944.

The onset of winter in 1944 brought a whole new dimension to armoured warfare in the northwest Europe campaign. The bad weather also masked a massive German build-up and kept the Allied air forces grounded for long periods of time. In the meantime the Allied armies were lulled into a false sense of security – little did they know that Hitler had been rebuilding his panzer armies.

With an M10 tank destroyer on guard vehicles of the US 99th Infantry Division pass through Wirtzfeld en route to Elsenborn. They had no idea that they lay directly in the path of the 12th SS Panzer Division's attack on 16 December 1944, which formed part of Hitler's Ardennes offensive.

US troops on patrol in the heavy winter snows. The US 99th Infantry were well dug in before the Elsenborn ridge line and, along with the US 741st Tank Battalion and the 612th/613th Tank Destroyer Battalions, were to halt the SS panzers dead in their tracks.

More US troops queuing for 'chow' – the winter conditions made the fighting particularly difficult for both the infantry and tank crews.

A GI inspects a Panther that was flipped by the blast that destroyed it. Panthers and Jagdpanthers were used to attack the twin villages of Krinkelt and Rocherath during 17-18 December 1944. American bravery ensured that they did not break through.

Another Panther, this time outside the Hotel des Ardennes in Echternach. This vehicle's superstructure has been partially hidden by the heavy snows.

A captured Sherman used by the Germans, but denied to Panzer Brigade 150, abandoned round the back of the Hotel des Ardennes. German efforts to create a unit equipped with Allied armour failed miserably.

American bodies by the Bullingen and Losheimergraben road junction to the south-east of the Elsenborn ridge. They were killed during the attacks launched by the 12th Volksgrenadier Division. The Germans greatly underestimated the Americans' ability to stand up to their panzers in this sector.

Very young and very tired-looking teenagers captured from the 12th SS Panzer Division. The youth on the right looks bemused and bewildered. However, both still have an air of defiance about them. Their youth shows that by this stage of the war the German Army was really scraping the barrel for recruits.

On 21 December 1944 the 12th SS's attacks were finally halted by the heavily armed M36 Gun Motor Carriage of the 613th Tank Destroyer Battalion. This utilised an M10/M4A3 Sherman chassis, fitted with an open-top turret armed with a 90mm gun. This was capable of tackling both the Tiger and Panther at long range. The vehicle seen here in the Ardennes is its smaller cousin the M18 Hellcat GMC, armed with a 76mm gun and specializing in 'hit and run tactics.' Hellcats equipped US tank destroyer battalions in northern Europe, where their speed and firepower made them very effective.

Spent US artillery shell cases on the Elsenborn Ridge. The last German attack on 22 December 1944 was met by a deluge of 10,000 rounds. Successful German inroads further south soon wilted in the face of such Allied firepower.

Heavy American artillery such as this massive 240mm (9.5in) M1 howitzer was instrumental in breaking up the panzer attacks. The shockwave alone from such enormous shells was capable of taking a tank out.

Likewise, the US 203mm (8in) M1 howitzer could produce equally devastating results. The tracked tractor is an M4, of which 5,500 were built between 1943-45, and was designed for towing heavy artillery in the 90mm to 240mm range. The larger M6 tractor was built in much fewer numbers.

These abandoned German vehicles are Flakpanzer IVs known as the Wirbelwind. This consisted of a Panzer IV chassis fitted with an open-top turret, armed with a quad 20mm anti-aircraft gun. Judging by the charring on the first vehicle it was set on fire by its crew. In the autumn of 1944 production of the Wirbelwind ceased as the 20mm flak gun was not as effective as the 37mm flak gun fitted to the Flakpanzer IV Ostwind. Both were also used in a ground support role.

US troops unmask one of the Panthers masquerading as an American tank. Panzer Brigade 150 resorted to such measures in part because most German units with captured American tanks refused to give them up. This tank threw a track and was picked off. Note the tow cable attached to the front.

Another knocked out Panther pretending to be an American tank destroyer. Up close this deception fooled no one. Otto Skorzeny complained they would only 'deceive very young American troops seeing them at night from very far away.' The added panels on the turret did give it a passing resemblance to the US M10, however.

A Sturmgeschütz sporting an Allied recognition star belonging to Skorzeny's Kampfgruppe Y beside the N32 at Géromont. American sappers found it had been booby-trapped by its fleeing crew in a last gesture of defiance.

A knocked out Tiger II. During the Battle of the Bulge these tanks were unable to operate as long-distance killers in the confines of the Ardennes. As a result their performance was largely disappointing.

This snowbound Tiger II was knocked out by fighter-bombers and subsequently attracted this American squad's attention. No damage is readily visible so it may be that the crew simply fled. The Tiger II ended up being used in a defensive role, whereas it was intended as a breakthrough tank.

GIs in snow camouflage shelter behind a whitewashed Sherman near Bastogne.

The M16/M17 Multiple Gun Motor Carriage mounted four .50 calibre machine guns in the M3 and M5 half-track respectively. Anti-aircraft variants of the US half-track saw wide use with US forces throughout the northwest Europe campaign. This particular vehicle appears to be an M3 and is identifiable by the rounded mudguards.

This vehicle is a Jagdpanzer IV/70(V), a tank destroyer that went into production in August 1944. By December 137 were available for the Ardennes offensive. The superstructure has been torn from the chassis, and the three stripes on the barrel indicate that it accounted for three Allied tanks before it was destroyed.

The shattered remains of a StuG III, abandoned in a river, photographed in December 1944. This is probably the Ausf G, of which over 7,700 were built. A catastrophic explosion blew the top right off the superstructure, exposing the remains of the fighting compartment.

Men of the US 75th Infantry Division peer into a Kubelwagen belonging to the 2nd SS Panzer Division at Beffe, south of Liège, Belgium, on 7 January 1945. Further up the road is a Sherman M4A3(76)W belonging to the US 4th Cavalry Group.

Germans who died when the US 509th Parachute Infantry Battalion, with the US 3rd Armored Division, clashed with the 1st and 2nd Battalion of the 25th SS Panzergrenadier Regiment, 12th SS Panzer Division. This photo was taken on 29 December 1944.

The Ardennes offensive was very much a last gasp for Hitler's panzers on the Western Front and cost him dearly in men and materiel. These men suffered cold, miserable deaths far from home.

The M24 Chaffee light tank was first delivered to American tank battalions in late 1944 to replace the M5. It proved to be a fast and efficient reconnaissance vehicle.

Chapter Seven

Churchills in the Reichswald

Operation Veritable was designed to drive the Germans back and occupy the ground between the Maas and Rhine rivers. This heavily forested region greatly favoured the defenders, as did the soft ground and local floodwaters. Once again this terrain was highly unfavourable to the conduct of massed armoured warfare. Delays in launching the American southern pincer against the Siegfried Line gave the enemy precious time to prepare for the Anglo-Canadian attack. The Germans, whose three lines of defences were anchored on Schottheide, Cleves and Goch, were determined not to give up the west bank of the Rhine, which behind the Reichswald, running from Nijmegen to Calcar, was completely flooded.

The Canadian 1st Army was directed to attack along the northern flank while the British 2nd Army, supported by the Guards and 11th Armoured Divisions, were to punch their way through the Reichswald to the Rhine.

The US 9th Army was to conduct Operation Grenade, the southern element of the assault. German formations defending the area were a mixture of infantry and paratroops; the only armoured units which were held in reserve were the battered 116th and 15th Panzergrenadier Divisions with just ninety tanks between them.

Following the Ardennes offensive in late 1944, the Colmar pocket, way to the south, unnecessarily distracted Eisenhower's attention. During late January and early February 1945 French and American forces attacked General Siegfried Rasp's 19th Army trapped around Colmar. Although the pocket was sealed by 9 February and the Germans lost 22,000 PoWs, the bulk of the 19th Army escaped over the Upper Rhine.

In preparation for the advance of Montgomery's 21st Army Group (Canadian 1st, British 2nd and US 9th Armies), the Allied air forces sought to disrupt communications within the German industrial region of the Ruhr and between the Ruhr and the rest of Germany with Operation Bugle. Significantly these air attacks helped ensure that much of Field Marshal Model's Army Group B, consisting of General Hasso von Manteuffel's 5th Panzerarmee and General Gustav von Zangen's 15th Army, remained trapped in the Ruhr.

On 8 February Montgomery launched Veritable, his usual set-piece plodding battle, thrusting the Canadian 1st Army under Lieutenant General Sir Henry Crerar in the Netherlands, supported by the British 2nd Army under Lieutenant General Sir Miles Dempsey, into the Rhineland. The attack by 30th Corps involved three British and two Canadian infantry divisions supported by the Guards Armoured Division. Success relied on surprise and the weather. Massing tanks, other vehicles and guns in the Nijmegen area was no easy feat. General Horrocks recalled:

> Thirty-five thousand vehicles were used to bring up the men and their supplies. One million, three hundred thousand gallons of petrol were required. Five special bridges had to be constructed over the Maas. One hundred miles of road must be made or improved.

Over 1,000 tanks were gathered for the Reichswald offensive. General Horrocks remembered

> When the attack was launched, 50,000 troops were on the start line, supported by 500 tanks and some 500 specially adapted tracked vehicles. In addition there were another 10,000 waiting to advance north-east, in order to secure the left bank, and another 15,000 frontline troops in reserve with over 500 tanks.

In the face of such strength it seemed that the Germans would be simply overwhelmed.

Attacking through the Reichswald, Horrocks's 30th Corps came up against General Alfred Schlemm's 1st Parachute Army. The German 84th Division was successfully forced out the way, but fierce resistance was encountered from the German 7th Parachute Division. While Horrocks was faced solely by German infantry and tough paratroops, he noted, 'It was estimated that the enemy also had three infantry and two panzer divisions in reserve available to intervene rapidly in the battle.'

The forest was not suitable for Horrocks's wheeled vehicles, let alone tracked, and there were no east-west roads of any note and only two north-south routes. This meant that the tanks were held back, leaving the infantry to conduct a major frontal assault following a huge aerial and artillery bombardment. On 9 February, the very day after Veritable commenced, the Germans blew the Roer dam and flooded the valley. It was a desperate act, but the Germans knew it would impede the Allies' armour. The bitter fighting lasted until 21 February, culminating in the capture of Goch. This was followed by Operation Blockbuster, which took the Canadians to the Rhine itself.

'From now on the battle developed into a slogging match as we inched our way forward through mud and rain,' recalled General Horrocks after the Germans breached the banks of the Rhine upstream. 'Slowly and bitterly we advanced through the mud supported by our superb artillery.'

The Americans hoped to launch Operation Grenade across the Roer to the south, but were delayed for two weeks by the flooding. Eleven days after Veritable commenced Lieutenant General William H. Simpson pushed his US 9th Army forward from Geilenkirchen to the Rhine around Dusseldorf. At the same time Lieutenant General Alexander M. Patch's US 7th Army advanced to the Upper Rhine.

After bitter resistance in the Reichswald had been overcome, the Allies regrouped before pushing on to the Hochwald forested ridge and Xanten to the east. Once the Roer floodwaters had gone down the US 9th Army was able to cross the Roer on 23 February. Of those German forces on the west bank of the Rhine 290,000 were captured. Such haemorrhaging of manpower could not go on indefinitely.

By 1945 the Germans, expecting a big Allied push over the Rhine, did everything they could to stiffen the defences of this vast natural barrier. Mine fields were strengthened, as were the bunker and trench complexes, as well as the gun pits. They thought the Allies would strike downstream of Emmerich, so General Johannes Blaskowitz, commander of Army Group H, deployed the stronger of his two armies, the 25th, under General Gunther Blumentritt, there. General Schlemm's battered 1st Parachute Army was left to cover the forty-five miles between Emmerich and Duisburg.

Schlemm's command considered itself an elite formation, but its courage was beginning to waver due to the lack of armour support. After the fierce battles in the Reichwald the *fallschirmjäger* were exhausted. By this stage of the war few of the *fallschirmjäger* had ever made a parachute drop and their ranks were fleshed out with drafted young men and personnel transferred from the Luftwaffe. Even so generally their morale was surprisingly high. The British had a healthy respect for these German troops in their distinctive rimless helmets.

'We felt quite a professional affection for these paratroops,' recalled Corporal Wingfield of the 7th Armoured Division. 'They were infantry-trained, liked to use their own initiative. They had the same system of "trenchmates." They fought cleanly and treated prisoners, wounded and dead with the same respect they expected from us. If our uniforms had been the same we would have welcomed them as kindred spirits.' After capturing Xanten on the west bank of the Rhine the brigadier commanding the 43rd Infantry Division ordered his men to salute the defeated *fallschirmjäger* as they filed past. By mid-February Montgomery was facing the remains of four parachute, three infantry and two panzer or panzergrenadier divisions.

It seemed to the Germans that the Allied resources and firepower were limitless. They also knew in the back of their minds that continued resistance was increasingly pointless. With the Red Army just thirty-five miles from Berlin, the fighting in the west seemed futile to many senior German officers. Following the German counter-attacks into the Ardennes and Alsace, reserves were now completely depleted. The remaining mobile reserve consisted of the 47th Panzer Corps, which comprised the 116th Panzer Division and the 15th Panzergrenadier Division. These sounded formidable, but they could scrape together just thirty-five panzers.

The general prognosis for the Wehrmacht was not good. On 23 March Montgomery summed up the situation:

> the enemy has lost the Rhineland, and with it the flower of at least four armies – the Parachute Army, 5th Panzer Army, 15th Army, and 7th Army; 1st Army, farther to the south, is now being added to the list. In the Rhineland battles, the enemy has lost about 150,000 prisoners, and there are many more to come; his total casualties amount to about 250,000 since 8 February.

British Churchill tanks photographed in December 1944, moving along the road north of the German town of Geilenkirchen, which lies just east of the Dutch border. It had been captured by the US 84th Infantry Division on 19 November as part of Operation Clipper conducted by British 30th Corps. The Allies were resisted by panzergrenadiers from the 9th Panzer and 15th Panzergrenadier Divisions. Note how the wartime censor has blanked out the divisional sign on the front of the lead tank.

A British column of Carriers, towing 6-pounder anti-tank guns, and jeeps enter the German town of Heinsberg, again just east of the Dutch border, in January 1945. The nearest Carriers appear to be the Universal model developed by Carden-Loyd and Vickers-Armstrong, while the one in the background is the larger Loyd, identifiable by the visible front axle, introduced by Vivian Loyd & Co. Other versions included the British-built Oxford, Canadian Windsor and the American T16.

British infantry moving up; they invariably bore the brunt of the fighting. The second man in is carrying the PIAT anti-tank weapon.

A knocked out StuG III somewhere in Belgium in early 1945. This assault gun proved to be an ideal defensive weapon, but the gun's limited traverse left it vulnerable in an offensive role. This vehicle seems to have been caught by Allied bombers or artillery fire.

Under new ownership: a Canadian tank crew take a Panther for a test drive at Wyler, Germany, on 9 February 1945. Both sides press-ganged captured equipment into service, but this only lasted as long as ammunition and spare parts were available. Also there was always the danger of drawing friendly fire.

Churchills in the Reichswald forest on 17 February 1945. The vehicle in the middle is either a Mk II Armoured Recovery Vehicle, which had a dummy turret and gun, or an Ark bridging vehicle. Tank crews greatly disliked operating in the confines of woods for fear of close-quarter ambush.

Members of the 51st (Highland) Infantry Division rebadging a requisitioned German Sd Kfz 251 half-track armoured personnel carrier. This went into production in 1943 and over 15,000 were built.

Highlanders struggle to free their Carrier from the mud. The going in the Reichswald was not suitable for wheeled vehicles, let alone tracked. Getting stuck could be a dangerous experience as it often attracted the attention of enemy gunners.

DUKWs wade through the flooded streets. Operation Veritable was launched on 8 February 1945. The following day the Germans blew the Roer dam to impede the Allied attack.

Cold and tired-looking Americans from the US 9th Infantry Division, supported by M4A3E2. This was an up armoured assault tank variant of the Sherman M4A3 and, because of its bulky appearance, was known unofficially as 'Jumbo'. While it sported armour ranging from 100-150mm thick, it was still armed with the standard 75mm gun. A few of these infantry support tanks were refitted with 76mm guns. These troops were photographed near the town of Rath during Operation Grenade, which took the US 9th Army over the Roer.

After clearing the Reichswald British troops of the Canadian 1st Army supported by Churchill tanks move to take Cleves (Kleve), the German fortress city guarding the approaches to the Ruhr. Again these men look exhausted.

British tank crew with an adopted Panther.

Two shots of a Jagdpanther destroyed by the Canadians during the battle for the Reichswald. This vehicle was well camouflaged, but lost both its tracks and received multiple hits. A solitary 88mm round has been stood in front of it. The Jagdpanther did not go into production until January 1944 and only 392 were ever produced, so they made little overall impact on the fighting.

Another knocked-out Jagdpanther, this time being examined by an American soldier. Although a highly effective tank destroyer on a one-to-one basis, they were too few in number to stem the Allied tide.

Sherman tanks of the Canadian 4th Armoured Division ready to advance near Sonsbeck, Germany, which lies south-east of Cleves, on 9 March 1945. It is possible they are being used as artillery to soften up enemy strongpoints.

Canadian troops stop to have a chat by their Carrier, apparently oblivious to the dead German solider lying to their left. Corpses were a daily sight and most soldiers became immune to their presence.

An American-built Weasel Cargo Carrier sporting a rather odd winter camouflage pattern.

Chapter Eight

Jagdtigers at Ramagen

While Operation Plunder was the key armoured assault across the Rhine, during the Malta Conference Eisenhower announced additional crossings south of the Ruhr. It was almost as if the Americans were intent on stealing Montgomery's thunder. They launched Operation Lumberjack using Lieutenant Courtney H. Hodge's US 1st Army and General George S. Patton's US 3rd Army, attacking between Koblenz and Cologne on 1 March 1945.

The plan was to barge Model's Army Group B back through the Eifel region to the Rhine. Six days later Hodges met his 7th Corps commander, General Collins, on the Rhine at Cologne. The US 3rd Armored Division drove the remnants of the 9th Panzer Division from the city, but the Hohenzollern Bridge was destroyed before it could be secured or crossed.

More importantly, just an hour to the south armoured Combat Command B of the US 9th Armored Division, supported by elements of the US 78th Infantry Division, reached Remagen at the same time. Dramatically they seized the Ludendorff railway bridge, one of the few remaining spans over the Rhine, before the Germans could blow it up. The Americans had secured a bridgehead two weeks before Montgomery was ready to go. Ironically this bridge had originally been constructed during the First World War to move men and materiel to the Western Front. The bridge had two railway lines and a footpath, but one line had been boarded over to allow road traffic. The Americans wanted Lieutenant General William H. Simpson's US 9th Army to cross at Urdingen, but Montgomery refused, perhaps smarting because he had lost the opportunity to breach the Rhine defences first.

These operations served to distract the Germans southward. Lieutenant General Fritz Bayerlein, commanding the German 53rd Corps, wanted to gather three divisions before counter-attacking at Remagen, but Hitler gave orders for immediate attacks with everything to hand. On 10 March the newly formed 512th Heavy Tank Destroyer Battalion was thrown at the bridgehead. It was one of only two units equipped with the mighty Jagdtiger, which although armed with a formidable 128mm gun was unwieldy to operate. The 512th were unsuccessful, as were elements of 9th Panzer, and were used to cover the German withdrawal.

Ten days after its capture the battered Ludendorff Bridge fell into the Rhine killing twenty-eight American soldiers. Its loss mattered little, as by the 21st the Americans had five pontoon bridges over the Rhine at Remagen. However, its capture cost Field Marshal von Rundstedt his job as commander in the West. Albert Kesselring replaced him, who although a very able general who had fought with skill in Italy, found that there was little he could do to restore the deteriorating situation.

On 13 March Patton's 3rd Army crossed the Moselle, then, on the night of the 22nd, he further stole Montgomery's thunder by throwing the US 5th Infantry Division across the Rhine at Nierstien and Oppenheim south-west of Frankfurt. As part of the preparations the US 249th Engineer Battalion was given special training on the floating Bailey bridge in Trier. 'On 19 March, our headquarters was at Adenau, Germany,' recalled Captain John K. Addison of the 249th, 'where we were alerted to join the engineer task force for the Rhine crossing at Oppenheim. We would man the assault boats for the crossing of the second wave of the 5th Infantry Division, to be followed with the construction of the heavy pontoon bridge.'

German resistance to the crossing was negligible. 'Our engineer work went off like clockwork,' adds Captain Addison, 'although one raft was sunk, two of our men were lost, and as many as 200 Germans drowned. The sinking was caused by the sudden shifting of passenger weight brought on by panic.' Hitler immediately declared this a greater threat than the Remagen bridgehead, as this section of the Rhine was virtually unguarded. Hitler wanted to send a panzer brigade, but all that were available were five disabled Jagdtigers at the tank depot at Sennelager. By the evening of the 24th Patton had captured 19,000 prisoners.

South of Koblenz, at 0200 on 26 March, Patton's US 8th Corps pushed the US 89th and 87th Divisions across the Rhine at Boppard and St Goar. The powerful 89th was supported by the US 748th Tank and the 811th Tank Destroyer Battalions. Altogether the division plus supporting and attached forces numbered well over 23,000 men. To oppose them were Luftwaffe anti-aircraft battalions fighting as infantry and Volkssturm home guard, equipped with small arms, machine guns, 20mm and 88mm anti-aircraft guns, some field artillery and a few panzers.

The 354th and 353rd Infantry Regiments spearheaded the crossing. The 1st Battalion, 354th attacked towards Wellmich and the 2nd towards St Goarshausen from St Goar. Over a company and a half of 1st Battalion reached the east bank on the first wave with little resistance, but once ashore they came under heavy fire from the hillside behind Wellmich. German machine-gun and 20mm AA fire, along with the swift current, prevented the assault boats from returning to the west bank.

The 2nd Battalion, on the way over, were greeted with point-blank grazing fire just above the waterline. Nonetheless, a pontoon bridge was completed between St Goar and St Goarshausen the following day, allowing the tanks to cross, and over 2,700 prisoners were eventually taken. Further south Lieutenant General Patch's US 7th Army crossed the Rhine at Worms on 26 March, allowing a break-out towards Darmstadt.

American troops on parade just before the Rhine crossing. There was great rivalry amongst the Allies as to who would be first over: some American generals felt that there was too much dithering on the part of Montgomery.

In reality, getting over the Rhine was a major logistical problem. Those bridges not brought down by Allied bombers had been demolished by the retreating Germans. The only remaining bridge that Allied armour could use was the Ludendorff railway bridge at Remagen.

An American column led by a Weasel cargo carrier moves through a devastated town. The amphibious variant proved very valuable.

GIs marching through a section of the Siegfried Line, which ran from Cleves, on the border with the Netherlands, along the German border all the way to Switzerland. Note the girders at the roadside: these slotted into the teeth of the concrete gateway to obstruct Allied tanks. Concrete 'Dragon's Teeth' can also be seen to the right.

American artillery moving up to the front. The first, a 105mm, is sporting Tunisian and Sicilian battle honours: 'Djebel, Berda and Mt Etna'. The heavy field gun in the second image is being towed by an M5 artillery tractor, which was introduced in 1943 with 5,290 built by the end of the war.

Troops from the US 90th Infantry Division crossing the Mosel River at Hatzenport, Germany, just south of Koblenz on 14 March 1945. This illustrates just how exposed the men were to enemy fire when using these open assault boats.

Two knocked-out panzers. The first is almost certainly a Panzer Mk IV Ausf H, one of the later production models, though it has the wire mesh skirts rather than the Schürzen steel plates normally associated with the Ausf J (which had three instead of four return rollers). The second tank is a Panzer Mk V Ausf G Panther. After Hitler's Ardennes offensive his panzer forces were largely spent and those that were still available were sent to the Eastern Front to try and slow down the advance of the Red Army.

On 7 March 1945, as part of Operation Lumberjack, elements of the US 9th Armored Division captured the Ludendorff bridge over the Rhine at Remagen. Sergeant Alexander A. Drabik became the first American soldier to cross the Rhine into Germany. The German garrison consisted of just thirty-five men.

General Patton on the Rhine. He managed to steal Montgomery's thunder by getting his men over the river first.

Hitler's paucity of panzers in northwest Europe meant he struggled to gather sufficient forces for a counterattack at Remagen. On 10 March 1945 lumbering Jagdtigers of the newly formed 512th Heavy Tank Destroyer Battalion were hastily thrown against the American bridgehead with predictable results.

With only two bridges remaining over the Rhine at Wesel and Remagen, the Allies had no choice but to rely on pontoon bridges to get their armour over. However, they had to capture the far bank.

An American M4A2 or A3(76mm) Sherman rumbles through the outskirts of the German city of Cologne. The US 3rd Armored Division drove the remnants of the 9th Panzer Division from the city on 7 March 1945, but the Hohenzollern Bridge was destroyed before it could be captured.

In the first shot a GI stands guard over a destroyed Panther from 9th Panzer in the middle of Cologne. The second photo appears to be the same tank. Evidently from the warning poster the temptation of the cathedral was too much for some, with fatal results.

Yet another knocked-out Panther. By this stage the panzer divisions had lost most of their coherence and fought on bravely as small tactical units.

German refugees at the Cologne railway station being questioned by American troops from the US 1st Army.

More German civilians, this time being searched in the city of Kreifeld in early March 1945.

The Rocket Launcher T34 Calliope on an M4. This consisted of sixty 4.6in rocket tubes mounted in a frame above the turret. The two bottom sets of tubes could be jettisoned on all variants except the M4A1. This was first used by the US 2nd Armored Division in France in August 1944. It saw limited combat until the end of the war.

A Sherman M4A3(76)W from the 14th Armored Division in Rittershoffen, Alsace, north-eastern France, in March 1945. The crew have piled sandbags around the hull to try and give the tank some additional protection from the Panzerfaust, the German answer to the bazooka.

Men of the US 78th Infantry Division pass two knocked-out Jagdpanzer 38(t) Hetzers from the 272nd Panzerjäger Battalion in Ketsenich on the German border with Belgium in late January 1945. The Hetzer went into production in April 1944 and 2,500 were built before the war ended.

Chapter Nine

Baileys on the Rhine

The things were noisy; there was no way of masking them; with the British Buffalo Landing Vehicle Tracked there was no element of surprise, though Montgomery had a good go at trying. The banks of the Rhine were shrouded in a thick man-made fog; this may have visually concealed things, but from the racket it was clear to the Germans that an awful lot of mechanized vehicles were being brought up to various jump-off points. On the night of 23 March 1945 the Allies crossed Germany's last major defensive barrier and after Operation Overlord this was the second largest operation undertaken by the British Army during the entire war.

The logistics were staggering. As well as the amphibious Buffalo there were also landing craft, powered rafts, 6x6 DUKWs, 8x8 Terrapins, tracked Weasels and DD Sherman swimming tanks gathered for the Rhine crossing. Forty-five medium landing craft and a similar number of landing craft vehicle personnel were shipped to Ostend from Britain. Under their own power they then made their way to Antwerp and were picked up by Army transporters for the onward journey. To many it must have looked like D-Day all over again.

The lead assault formation was Major General Sir Percy Hobart's British 79th Armoured Division, affectionately known as the 'Funnies' because of its unique armour. This division had served the Allies well on D-Day and ever since. It consisted of five brigades operating almost 2,000 specialized vehicles and gun tanks, including approximately 500 Buffaloes, which were allocated to the various assault infantry divisions. In addition about 100 DD Sherman tanks were to support the initial waves, while eight Class 50/60 rafts were to ferry over almost 800 tanks. Some 200 DUKWs were refurbished by the British ready for the Rhine operation. In stark contrast the weak 47th Panzer Corps was the Germans' only mobile reserve, and in the face of Allied air supremacy it was hardly capable of going anywhere without being met by a hail of rockets and bombs.

Despite their massed power the Rhine crossing presented particular problems for the Allied planners, not least the steep and very muddy river banks. To counter this hard-won lessons from the Scheldt were called upon. The Buffalo Carpet-Layer was developed after fourteen Sherman DD tanks had become stuck fast in the mud during the assault on South Beveland. The net result was that they and their crews had become sitting ducks and they had been unable to support the assaulting infantry. For the assault over the Rhine Special Buffalo Troops were to lay chespale wooden carpeting to assist the supporting tanks up and over the banks.

In total Montgomery's 21st Army Group could call on 1.2 million men of General Crerar's Canadian 1st Army (consisting of eight divisions), General Dempsey's British 2nd Army (eleven divisions including three armoured and two airborne,) and General Simpson's US 9th Army (eleven divisions including three armoured). For ten days before the crossing Montgomery's gathering forces at Wesel were shrouded in a dense choking smokescreen, making it obvious that something was about to take place. The Allied logistical effort was huge, involving 59,000 British and American engineers. The British 2nd Army drew an additional 118,000 tons of stores, including 60,000 tons of ammunition, while the US 9th drew an extra 138,000 tons of stores.

First into battle were the men of the 51st Highland Division, which had been strengthened by the addition of the 9th Canadian Infantry Brigade. Major-General Tom Rennie was supported by 150 Buffaloes, which carried his four assault battalions. The Buffaloes ploughed resolutely through the Rhine's strong current, but the DUKWs struggled in many places and often ended up on the wrong stretch of bank. All the DD tanks of the Staffordshire Yeomanry were across by 0700 and in action engaging enemy strongpoints.

The Black Watch took just four minutes to cross and were the first British troops over. The defenders, stunned by the preceding bombing and artillery attacks, offered sporadic mortar and machine-gun fire in response to the forces ploughing toward them. Remarkably, the 7th Black Watch lost just one Buffalo in the opening attack, to a German Teller mine. The commanding officer of the 4th Battalion, Royal Tank Regiment was in the first Buffalo to reach the opposite bank on 23 March at 2104.

At Xanten the assault battalions encountered a stone-lined bank, which their Buffaloes could not climb, and the units became widely scattered. Fortunately, this obstacle proved to be the only serious difficulty as the German defenders put up little resistance. The ground north-east of Rees was quickly secured, but German paratroops resolutely held onto the town until the next day.

The 43rd Division then moved up on the 51st's left to attack Esserden, while the 9th Canadian Infantry Brigade pushed on Androp and Bienen, reaching Emmerich by the 27th. The 3rd Canadian, 15th (Scottish), 43rd, 51st (Highland) Divisions and the equipment of the 6th Airborne Division were ferried across by 425 Buffaloes. They made almost 4,000 crossings, with fifty-five damaged and nine written off; not a bad casualty rate for such an enormous operation.

On the 25th Churchill and Montgomery arrived at Eisenhower's HQ. Following lunch they went to a house on the Rhine to look at a quiet German sector. After Eisenhower had gone the pair could not resist crossing with a group of American officers, remaining in enemy territory for thirty minutes. During a later visit to the destroyed Wesel railway bridge they were driven away by German artillery; Churchill was in his element.

At 1800 on the 25th the Americans drove the 116th Panzer Division from Hunxe. The following day the panzers initially found themselves holding the entire 47th Panzer Corps front until assisted by the 180th and 190th Infantry Divisions. To the south the German 53rd Corps, consisting of the 2nd Parachute and 'Hamburg' Divisions, struggled to hold their defences. The latter unit was made up of staff and communications personnel supported by some paratroops.

By the afternoon of the 26th the four Class 50/60 rafts on 12th Corps' front had ferried over about 250 tanks, while on 30th Corps' front another four rafts had shifted 437 tanks by the 27th. During the night of 27/28 the remains of 116th Panzer withdrew under covering fire from the divisional artillery. Montgomery then prepared to commit his other four Corps and by the 26th seven 40-ton bridges had been put over the Rhine. The logistics of bridging the Rhine were mind-boggling. To get the Allied armoured fighting vehicles and motor transport over the river required 22,000 tons of assault bridging including 25,000 wooden pontoons, 2,000 assault boats, 650 storm boats and 120 river tugs.

This allowed the British 12th Corps' 7th Armoured Division under Major General L.O. Lyne and the US 16th Corps' 8th Armored Division under Brigadier General John M. Devine to move into the bridgehead. There was no stopping these formations and by midnight on 28 March the bridgehead had expanded considerably. The 7th Armoured thrust forward as far as Borken, some twenty miles, and the 8th Armored got to Haltern at about twenty-five miles. Everywhere the exhausted German units struggled to put up a coherent defence, but the lack of panzers with which to conduct counter-attacks left them simply plugging holes in their line as they appeared.

By early 1945 the battered German Army was in full-scale retreat. This RAF reconnaissance photo shows German vehicles nose-to-tail streaming west to east across the Duisburg-Homberg road bridge over the Rhine on 4 March. In assessing the German defences General Horrocks observed: 'Behind in immediate reserve were our old friends, or enemies, 15th Panzergrenadier Division and 116th Panzer Division.' The truth was that these units had few if any panzers.

One of the Germans' few remaining Panther tanks, photographed in early 1945. The sheer volume of Allied armour would soon overwhelm it. The crew must have appreciated that it was only a matter of time before the Allies would storm the Rhine and be in the very heart of Germany.

The shattered remaines of the city of Wesel. From mid-February to mid-March RAF Bomber Command and the US 8th and 9th Air Forces conducted 16,000 sorties, dropping almost 50,000 tons of bombs on German defences. The garrison was also attacked at low level, and from 11-21 March the British 2nd Tactical Air Force and the US 24th Tactical Air Command flew 7,300 sorties. The Germans were granted just two days to catch their breath before, at 1700 on 23 March, the Allied artillery bombardment began and continued until 0945 the following morning.

Ungainly Buffaloes carrying ambulances en route to the Rhine crossings. Around 500 Bufflaoes were deployed in support of the operation, which included a carpet-laying variant. On the eve of the crossing Montgomery signalled: 'Over the Rhine, then, let us go. And good hunting to you all on the other side.'

DD swimming tanks crossing the Rhine. One hundred of these supported the initial assault. Also 700 tanks were ferried over by eight Class 50/60 rafts. Although the DD tank presented a small target, this shot shows how vulnerable the crews were.

British troops, fully laden with their kit, plough across the Rhine in a Buffalo. The 3rd Canadian, 15th (Scottish), 43rd, 51st (Highland) Divisions and the equipment of the 6th Airborne Division were ferried across by 425 Buffaloes. Losses of this amphibious vehicle were surprisingly low.

More Buffaloes in the Rhine. They made almost 4,000 trips with fifty-five damaged and nine written off. While its maximum speed on land was 25mph, in the water it could only manage 7mph. The flat bow visible in the second photo shows how it simply bludgeoned its way through the water.

This shot shows clearly just how low the Buffalo was in the water. Note the offset box shield for the .30 inch calibre machine guns. Initially the exposed gunners were not given any protection, but eventually various patterns of gunshield were provided.

Soldiers of the 15th (Scottish) Infantry Division scramble from their assault boat after crossing the Rhine and make their way up the east bank to an assembly point near Xanten. Although wet and tired this was no time to linger.

Members of the British 1st Commando Brigade in the devastated outskirts of Wesel.

A British M10 roars past Allied gliders. By 25 March 1945 British forces had linked up with the airborne troops and the US 9th Army establishing a continuous 21st Army Group bridgehead some thirty miles long and seven miles deep. The airborne assault opened at 1000 on 24 March, using the British 6th Airborne Division and the US 17th Airborne Division. The Germans had anticipated a major airborne drop deep in their rear at the same time as the crossing. They were therefore thrown by Operation Varsity not being simultaneous and barely five miles beyond the Rhine.

M4 Shermans of the US 781st Tank Battalion just before the Rhine crossing.

American infantry coming under intense small arms fire on the Rhine. These men are from the US 89th Infantry Division, which was supported by the US 748th Tank and 811th Tank Destroyer Battalions, crossing at St Goar on 26 March 1945.

American armour being ferried over the Rhine by landing craft. The first shot shows an M24 Chaffee light tank, the second an M4 Sherman medium tank. The Allied build-up once over the Rhine was quite remarkable.

British Prime Minister Winston Churchill with Field Marshal Montgomery just to his right on the east bank of the Rhine on 25 March 1945. Churchill, with one eye always on historic moments, could not resist being present. In secret he flew to Montgomery's HQ near Velno to watch the beginning of operations Plunder and Varsity. On the 25th he and Montgomery arrived at Eisenhower's HQ. Following lunch they went to a house on the Rhine to look at a quiet German sector. After Eisenhower had gone the pair could not resist crossing with a group of American officers, remaining in enemy territory for thirty minutes. During a later visit to the destroyed Wesel railway bridge they were driven away by German artillery.

A British carrier about to cross a Bailey or pontoon bridge over the Rhine. Once these bridges were in position there was no stopping the Allied armoured divisions.

The US 9th Army crosses the Rhine via a steel treadway pontoon bridge built by the US 7th Armoured Engineer Battalion. Note the steel cabling either side holding it in place against the strong current. By the far bank the bridge has clearly kinked due to the immense pull of the water.

YOU ARE NOW CROSSING THE RHINE RIVER THROUGH COURTESY OF E CO. 17 ARMD ENGR BN AND C CO 202 ENGR C. BN

British troops fighting on the streets of Kervenheim in the Rhineland in March 1945. Despite all being lost the Germans fought doggedly on.

American soldiers pinned down on Nibelungen bridge in the city of Worms on 28 March 1945. The man in the foreground did not make it to cover in time and was killed by a sniper on the far bank of the Rhine. The ornate gothic tower where he is probably hiding has been damaged by shellfire.

Chapter Ten

Scrap Metal in the Ruhr

With the Allies swarming over the Rhine there was very little the Germans could do to contain them. Hitler hoped to counter-attack at every turn, but the units he was looking at were just flags in maps. Within a week of the crossing Montgomery had amassed twenty divisions with 1,500 tanks. There was simply nothing the Germans could do to withstand this steamroller and 30,000 PoWs went into the 'bag' after they threw down their weapons. In addition other elements of the British 2nd Army and Canadian 1st Armies were pushing into northern Germany and southern Holland. The US 9th Army struck south into the northern end of the Ruhr between Duisburg and Essen. The German defence was completely shattered.

Nonetheless, the panzers continued to resist to the very last, despite it being clear that all was now completely lost. Small units consisting of a handful of tanks and assault guns contested the Allied advance at every road junction, even in the confines of German cities, in a desperate bid to slow down their enemies. Valiantly the crews would fire off their last remaining rounds, then set fire to their vehicles and fight on as infantry. There was no questioning their professionalism.

Major Peter Carrington of the Guards Armoured Division was full of praise for his opponents, recalling:

> The Germans were very, very good soldiers. After the Rhine crossing, we had 15th Panzergrenadier Division in front of us fighting a rearguard action all the way to the very end of the war; in circumstances in Germany when they must have known they were going to lose the war and didn't have much hope. They fought absolutely magnificently with great courage and skill.

General Bayerlein, commanding 53rd Panzer Corps, was ordered on 29 March 1945 to try and break out eastwards with the remains of the Panzer Lehr, 9th Panzer, 3rd Panzergrenadier and 3rd Parachute Divisions. This represented the Germans' last major offensive in the west. Bayerlein's few remaining operational panzers lacked fuel and ammunition and by 2 April they were back where they started, driven back by overwhelming American firepower. The few panzers he had been able to muster were left as blazing wrecks. It was a depressingly futile gesture, but what could they do other than follow orders? General Blummentritt, commander of the 25th Army, felt it his duty to save the men under his command and withdrew behind the Ems Canal toward the cover of the Teutoburger Forest.

Further south the US 1st Army broke out of the Remagen bridgehead, while the spearhead of the US 9th and 1st Armies (the 8th Armored Division and Major General Maurice Rose's US 3rd Armored Division) linked up on 2 April at Lippstadt east of the Ruhr. Everywhere you looked Allied tanks drove the scattered enemy back.

The remnants of Field Marshal Model's Army Group B, some nineteen shattered divisions, from the 5th Panzerarmee and 15th Army, along with 63rd Corps from the broken 1st Parachute Army, were caught in the Ruhr pocket. Grandly Hitler dubbed it the 'Ruhr fortress': he saw it as a Nazi bastion upon which the Allied tide would flounder. The reality was a little different and final defeat was only a matter of time. The Allies, meantime, pushed on to meet up with the Red Army on the Elbe. The Buffaloes' swansong was ferrying Allied troops over the Elbe in late April/early May just before the German surrender.

The German forces caught in the Ruhr pocket were left to the specially created US 15th Army, consisting of eighteen divisions from the US 1st and 9th Armies, whose job was to mop up. German resources and energy were spent and the outcome was inevitable. Both the 9th and 116th Panzer Divisions surrendered to the Americans in mid-April. On 21 April 1945 Major General Joseph Harpe, commanding the 5th Panzerarmee, finally surrendered along with 325,000 men including twenty-nine generals. The Allies found that it was a panzer army only in name. The war in northwest Europe was over.

What must these German schoolchildren have thought? An American column led by a fuel tanker and trailer rumbles over a pontoon bridge at Worms. Once the Allied tanks were over the Rhine there was little the panzers could do to keep them out of Germany.

A blazing Tiger I typifies the end of the panzers. By this stage in the war most of the experienced crews were dead or wounded. Exposed in the middle of a German street this Tiger would have been easy prey for superior Allied firepower. It was either abandoned by its crew and set alight or caught in the rear by a stalking enemy tank as it withdrew.

One of the few new Allied tank designs introduced in the closing days of the war. This is the British Comet, which was first issued to the 11th Armoured Division after the Rhine crossing in March 1945. Armed with a 77mm gun, it proved to be reliable and fast and was the first British tank capable of matching the Panther, but its late arrival meant it did not play a prominent role in British tank actions.

Men of the 11th Armoured Division taking on ammunition for their Comet, photographed on 13 April 1945. Although called the Ordnance Quick Firing (OQF) 77mm Mk2, the gun was actually of 76.2mm calibre but was dubbed a 77mm to avoid confusion with the 17-pounder.

More British armour: this time a British Sherman Firefly armed with the 17-pounder gun, an M3 half-track, at least four Carriers and what appears to be a Humber armoured car. Armoured columns such as this became commonplace all over Germany.

Once the Allies' tanks were on the German autobahns there was little to impede their rapid progress. This tank is an M4A1 (76mm) Sherman with a cast hull and behind it is an M7 Howitzer Motor Carriage.

The M24 Chaffee light tank was another late entrant to the war, although by June 1945 4,070 had been built. American tank battalions first received it in late 1944 when it replaced the M5 and it came into increasing use in the closing months of the war, proving very popular with its crews.

Closing in on the Third Reich. Fighting its way down a German street is an M4A3(76mm) HVSS and its supporting infantry. Tanks were always vulnerable to concealed anti-tank weapons, especially the hand-held Panzerfaust and the Raketenpanzerbuchse, in such built-up areas.

A German staff car at the bottom of a smashed reinforced steel and concrete autobahn bridge. The second shot shows the makeshift wooden bridge built alongside to replace it. Operation Bugle was an Allied air offensive designed to cut communications between the Ruhr and the rest of Germany in February 1945. It ensured that most of the German 5th Panzer Army and 15th Army were trapped in the Ruhr when the leading elements of the US 1st Army and US 9th Army met at Lippstadt in early April 1945.

The last of the Panzers. A Tiger I unceremoniously shunted off the road in the Ruhr pocket. There is a good chance that it simply ran out of fuel. The second photo shows a StuG III that fought and died at the road junction it was defending.

The Krupp armament works at Essen in the central Ruhr. The city was bombed over 270 times during the course of the war. Elements of the US 17th Airborne Division captured Essen on 19 April 1945 unopposed. The second two shots show British intelligence officers touring Krupp to assess the bomb damage and German production capabilities.

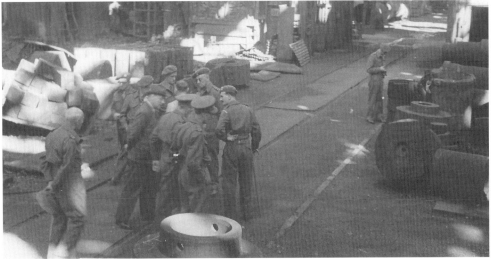

The face of defeat, though there is an air of relief that it is all over. Thousands of German PoWs crossing a pontoon bridge on the Elbe after three German divisions surrendered unconditionally to the British 2nd Army.

A knocked-out M4A3(76mm) HVSS belonging to the US 14th Armoured Division in Bavaria on 4 April 1945. By this stage German forces were left reeling everywhere.

A burning M4 Sherman belonging to the US 741st Tank Battalion, veterans of Normandy and the Elsenborn Ridge, on the streets of Leipzig. The entire crew were killed while supporting the US 2nd Infantry Division serving with the US 1st Army.

More US 1st Army armour on the streets of Leipzig, this time two M18 Hellcat Gun Motor Carriages. This proved to be one of the best tank destroyers of the Second World War, with a top speed of 50mph it was also the fastest AFV during 1944-45.

With hostilities over the crews of these M5 light tanks take it easy in the German sunshine.

With the panzers defeated the British and American armies found themselves sharing garrison duties with the Red Army in Berlin. On 21 June 1945 the British 7th Armoured Division took part in the 'End of the War Parade.'

A souvenir to take home.

Most of Hitler's panzers ended up in the scrapyard or sold to Arab armies in the Middle East. A French family pose by a captured Panther, a reminder of the bitter armoured warfare fought during the northwest Europe campaign of 1944-45.